BELL'

Famous JOE COSLEY

A Romantic, poetic Joe Cosley
Picture courtesy of Helen (Bouchard) Hinks

Brian McClung

What others are saying about:
Belly River's Famous JOE COSLEY

"I got so caught up in the sheer enjoyment of reading this book. It's a fascinating book about a Ranger in Glacier Park and lots of history all round the park. Keep up the great work!"

— Geneva (Beazer) Fellows

"Great Book! There can be little doubt that Joe Cosley is still the most famous rascal in Glacier Park History *and* the public favorite. The reason he was not more severely punished may be that so many others in the Park Service and among the local elite were probably doing pretty much the same thing that Cosley was, only Cosley was more organized."
— Jack Holterman, author of *Place Names of Glacier and Waterton National Parks* and *Let the Mountains Sing.*

"I grew up on my grandfather, J. J. West's stories of Joe Cosley and I really never knew what was fact and fiction. He was the Robin Hood of the Belly River Valley; a rogue, a romantic, and a robber. His education, artistic talent, and mountain man skills set him apart in this early frontier area. He was truly a unique individual worthy of an accurate and in-depth story of his life. It was a most enjoyable and enlightening story to read. Thanks, Brian."

— Richard West, Mountain View, Alberta

"Fascinating information! I gained a new understanding of the Cosley story. Good job!" — Bruce Fladmark, Cultural Resources Manager, Glacier National Park.

"Brian McClung has presented a well written, highly interesting, factual and well documented manuscript, the almost legendary Joe Cosley — pioneer trapper, naturalist, prospector, guide, raconteur, artist and writer of the Waterton Lakes / Glacier National Parks. I recommend this book as excellent reading for anyone interested knowing about Joe Cosley and "the way it was" in those early years."
— Frank Goble, author of Four books, *The Trapper, part 1, 2, and 3;* and *Bears I Have Known*

Dedication

We are dedicating this Third Edition to Joe Cosley's family and friends who he held in high regard. Just one example of this is his Military Will dated April 6, 1917. It reads to Mrs. Steven Cosley (Mother) My trunk containing clothes, six shooter and belt, 22 rifle, skates, photo album, all my horses (four in number)and half the increase. To his friends: William Webster – All my books, and half the increase of my horses and pack outfits, overcoat; Aunty T. Webster – my phonograph, all my records, one photo album and bedding; Miss Thirsa Webster - my typewriter; Miss Rebecca Webster - my camera, all my films and developing outfit; Willie Webster – my spurs and bridle; Ellis Webster – my hat; Susie (Keuly) Kenly – my picture of Edith Webster.

Living out West, far away from his family, friends became very important to Joe, almost like family. He made frequent visits to friends in Montana and Southern Alberta. Always a gracious guest, he would bring peppermint sticks to Herman Webster because Joe knew Herman like them. When visiting Bob and Thelma Lowe, Joe would always bring the hindquarters of a mountain sheep for Thelma to cook. It was a treat for everyone. Joe was well like by his friends and they looked forward to his visits.

Joe's friends were true friends. While Joe was hiding out at his camp, Laura Nelson took food and supplies to him at a pre-arranged spot in the Southern Alberta foothills. After his arrest, Duke Sanders and another friend rescued Joe's fur, traps and supplies.

A Special Thank you to my Sweet Marie

You are my traveling companion down all of life's trails. Your research and editing skills greatly improved this Second Edition. I am thrilled you married me and you still wear my diamond ring.

Along the Trail

Belly River's Famous Joe Cosley is the twin companion to ***Hooked for Good, Hooked for Life: The Passion for Fishing Belly River.***

Conceived together but delivered separately, the two books go hand in hand. Not identical, each book, with its own unique personality, encompasses the same Belly River system.

It is about the early history of the Belly River Ranger District in Glacier National Park and its connection to the surrounding towns on both sides of the border. Joe Cosley crossed the line in more ways than one. This book is about those who played a vital part in the early history of Glacier and Waterton Lakes National Parks.

Belly River's Famous Joe Cosley

By

Brian McClung

Published in 2010 by

Life Preservers Publishing LLC

2863 Jamie Rose Street

Las Vegas, NV 89135

First Printing 1998
Second Printing 2009: **Glacier National Park Centennial Limited Edition**
Revised by Brian and Marie McClung
Third Printing 2010, revised by Brian and Marie McClung
Front Cover Picture: Joe Cosley in his Glacier National Park uniform, 1910

McClung, Brian
Belly River's Famous Joe Cosley/ by Brian McClung

Third Edition

Includes bibliographical references:

1. Trapping and poaching – United States. 1. Title.
2. History of Glacier National Park – Montana
3. History of Waterton Lakes National Park – Alberta
4. Drawing wildlife and writing stories
5. Carving trees

CONTENTS

LIST OF ILLUSTRATIONS

Glossary

Names of places change over years. First, different people assign names to places and some of them stick and others don't.

PLACE NAMES

Belton:	West Glacier
Glacier Park:	East Glacier
H.Q.:	Glacier National Park Headquarters in Belton
Gt. NRR:	Great Northern Railway
North Fork	
Kennedy Creek:	Otatso Creek
Waterton RS	Goat Haunt Ranger Station in Glacier National Park
BB Flat:	Beebe Flats
Main:	Babb, Montana
NWT:	North West Territories: Alberta (1905)
Belley River:	Belly River (river and lakes)
Mokowanis:	Big Bellies: Belly River
Wests:	J.J. West: John J. West: John Jacob West: West's Ranch
GNP:	Glacier National Park with headquarters in Belton
GNP Waterton:	Goat Haunt Ranger Station
The Line:	Slash: US/Canada border: 25' strip cut through forest to mark the boundary.
Crossley:	Crosley: Cosley Lake: Cosley Ridge
Glense Lakes:	Glenns Lake
Apple Jack:	Brandy distilled from hard cider: any liquor
Secret Camp:	Cosley's trapline camp in Glacier National Park
Cosley Trees:	Trees that Joe Cosley carved his name or initials in
Cosley Trail:	Basically Lee Ridge then down to either Slide Lake or Belly River Ranger Station. Cosley had other trails he called his own that paralleled the Belly River Trail on the east side of the river.
Kootenay Lakes:	WNP: Waterton Lakes National Park
Midvale:	East Glacier

WARNING — DISCLAIMER

This book is published to provide the most exhaustive study about Joe Cosley. Please forgive, if you think I have omitted some material or a picture that you think I should have included.

It is sold with the understanding that the author and publisher are not engaged in rendering any professional services. If expert assistance is required, the help of competent professionals should be sought.

Every effort has been made to make this as complete and accurate as possible. However, there **may be mistakes,** both typographical and in content. This book is updated each printing. If you have any comments, corrections or additions — including any pictures or experiences you would like to share, please forward them with contact information.

Trapping is not a get-rich quick scheme. Anyone who decides to trap must expect to invest a lot of time and effort and ask permission to enter another's property.

The purpose of this book is to educate and entertain. The author and Life Preservers shall have neither liability nor responsibility to any person or entity with respect to loss or damage caused, or alleged to be caused, directly or indirectly by the information contained in this book. Don't use Ahern Pass. Be bear wise. Owning a copy of this book or reading someone else's, does not give you license to hunt or trap in Glacier or Waterton or any other national park today.

ACKNOWLEDGMENTS

I have not attempted to cite all the authorities and sources. To do so would require more space than is available. Scores of people contributed to this edition.

Owen McClung, my father knows lots of people and their facts and introduced me to Joe Heimes and several others.

My brother Lynn came through at a time I needed it the most – prior to a deadline. He is a great writer and editor in his own right.

I thank the following for their timely suggestions to this book: Joe Heimes, Marie McClung, Marge Wight, Geneva (Beazer) Fellows, Bud Spencer, Jack Holterman, Rob Watt, Richard and Daveeda West, Edwin Knox, Deirdra Shaw, Bruce Fladmark, Frank Goble, Dorothy Brading, and Linda Barron.

My sincere thanks to all these fine people. I know they are as proud of the part they have played in the development of highcountry Belly River as they are of their contribution to this work.

Historical Summary of Joe Cosley

Joe Cosley's age is so noted (19)

1870, May 24:	Joseph Clarence Cosley born in Ontario, Canada, father French , mother Algonquin Indian
1887	Oldest Cosley Trees in Kishenehn
1889, Nov 8:	Montana becomes the 41st state in the Union (19) Joe was in Kalispell for this celebration.
1890	Cosley said he worked with Lt. Ahern to build Pass Trail (20)
1891:	Cosley namesake on lake, ridge, claims naming others (21)
1895	Waterton Lakes National Park organized in Canada's North West Territories adjacent to 49th Parallel (25)
1897, Nov 09:	Oldest standing aspen tree in Waterton Lakes National Park which Cosley carved name, (27)
1900:	U. S. National Forest ranger (30)
1905,	Alberta was made the 7th Province of Canada (35)
1910:	Glacier National Park ranger (40) Ranger Cosley permanently assigned to Belly River (40)
1911:	Joe was discovered trapping at upper McDonald Lake, fired as ranger but Cosley returned to Belly River and all seemed to be forgotten (42)
1914, June:	The Park sent Ralph Thayer to fire Cosley, tells him to get out of the Park and his pay was cut off. (44)
1914, Aug:	Cosley first to join the 13th Mounted Rifles in Cardston, (44)
1916, Sum	Unit joins with Fort Gary Horse and sent to France. (46)
1919, Spr	Cosley returns to Cardston and guides in Glacier, continues to trap and poach in Glacier and Waterton Parks (48)
1926, Dec 5:	Joseph F. Heimes full time Ranger assigned permanently to Belly River district in GNP (56)
1929, May 6	Ranger Heimes arrests Cosley for poaching, possession of firearms, traps, pelts, and took Cosley to trial (58)
1929, May 10:	Friends of Cosley paid bail, Cosley released, snowshoes over Ahern Pass into Belly River and retrieves his cache of furs and traps in GNP and takes them into Canada (58)
1929, May 12	Took the furs to market in Canada before his birthday (58)
1943:	Joseph Clarence Cosley died of scurvy in a trapper's cabin in Northern Saskatchewan but was not found until 1944 (73)

I never met Joe Cosley. I wish I had. However, on my journey to discover more about him, I met lots of people who knew Cosley personally. The bonus was that each person knew him for more than just a week. It has been a double thrill to explore both Montana and Alberta and uncover new photographs of him and his famous story.

I hope you will enjoy reading about Cosley as much as I have had researching his life and times. It just may take you by surprise.

Belly River's Famous JOE COSLEY:

Mountain Man, Fancy Shooter, Ranger, Soldier, Indian Fighter, Renegade, A Man's Man, Artist, War Hero, Fancy Rider, Photographer, Newsmaker, Trapper, Poacher, Guide, Romantic, Poet, Fancy Skater, Writer, Tree Carver, Ladies Man And All Around Good Guy.

Joe Cosley posed for a staged camera shot at Main (Babb) Montana. Look how innocent and debonair he looks. He is making history in the Wild West. Notice the diamond hitch on the packhorse. Cosley was known for his speed in throwing a diamond hitch.
Picture courtesy of Glenbow Archives, Calgary, Alberta.

The saddle horse and packhorse outfit in this picture belonged to Joe Cosley. Notice the characteristic fancy saddle that looks like it was made from alligator hide. Perhaps the photographer suggested that Joe could not only have his picture taken with the staged setting, he could also include his two horses. He named his trusted mount, "Black Bess," and his packhorse, "Jingo."

Cosley rode and raced "Vassar," his previous horse in the late 1880's until the early 1900's. Some of the early pioneers in Southern Alberta report that Joe rode his horse with this fancy saddle and outfit in this part of the Northwest Territories in the early 1900's when he started working for the Forest Service. They also say Joe Cosley did some packing for miners.

Early records with Glacier state there was an Indian that helped build the Ahern Pass trail. Lt. George Patrick Ahern and his soldiers punched a trail north from Lake McDonald across the Continental Divide and down to Belly River.

Records mention that there was a half-breed Indian, by the name of Crossley, along with this pack train crew. This Crossley may have been "our Joe," a packer for Lt. Ahern.[1]

Ahern Pass is the most dangerous trail in Glacier National Park, "fit only for a crazy man."

The record also suggests that the Ahern pack train crossing of "Ahern Pass" was one of only two such crossings ever recorded. Those two were surveyor Sergent and packer Frank Valentine. That may be. However, once the Ahern was built Cosley used it regularly. Some Canadian ranchers also started using this pass to save days of extra travel to visit family and friends living south of the border.

Oaklie Thompson, still living, remembers that he, his dad Al, and some of the West boys traveled across Ahern Pass regularly during the 1920's. Their last trip across was in the early 1930's. Of course, by then, roads around the park made travel more accessible by automobile.

Joe Cosley sent this postcard to several personal friends on both sides of the border. He sent one to Kootenay Brown in Waterton and one to J. J. West in Mountain View, Alberta. He "kept in touch" by sending one to Charlie Howe at Apgar and to other friends in Columbia Falls, Montana. No doubt, he also sent the card to his family and maybe to your family as well.

There was a photographer that traveled all over the west, and came to Main, Montana annually. The locals knew when the next photo shoot would be and the word got around.

---

[1] Haney Vaught manuscript, GNP.

Over the years Cosley had his picture taken in different poses and had postcards made from the prints. Postcards were a standard option back then, much like Christmas Photo Cards are today.

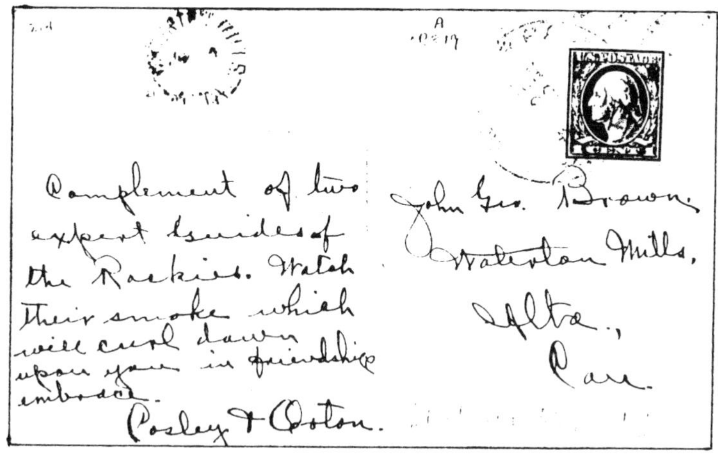
Complement of two expert Guides of the Rockies. Watch their smoke which will curl down upon you in friendship embrace.
Cosley & Coton.

John Geo. Brown,
Waterton Mills,
Alta.,
Can.

This postcard was addressed to John Geo. Brown, Waterton Mills,[2] Alta., Can. The note above postcard: *"Here is where friendship ceases and business commences"* Below: *"See America First"*

The message indicated Cosley's native roots in speaking of sacred smoke. Indians, mountain-men and squaw-men celebrate smoke. It was postmarked at Glacier Park (East Glacier today), Montana on June 29, 1910.

Joe was announcing that he was leaving the National Forest Service and becoming a Ranger with the National Park as one of nine original rangers. This meant increased prestige, a raise in pay, a better hat, new uniforms and equipment, new opportunities to make a name for himself and something to talk about for a lifetime.

It was business time.

---

[2] The main export from Waterton Park was not tourism; it was lumber. Frank Goble reports that, "Much of the early timber was harvested at the head of the upper lake in Montana. It was towed in a log boom down the lake by the Hanson steamer, "The Gertrude," to the sawmill at Waterton Mills, located at the Maskinonge just upstream from the present Waterton River bridge. Hanson had pilings in the river above the bridge and a log boom connected to the pilings and to each shore of the river to hold the logs until hauled out and stacked by the mill. Waterton Mills was the Post Office address. Kay Kenley told Frank Goble that the Hanson heirs still own the timber rights at the head of the lake, but not the surface rights, so they are prevented from logging the timber."

Joe Cosley's career was now galloping ahead and towering above anything he had ever accomplished.

He might have been thinking how far he had come out west in just two decades — not how far he had traveled to go west, rather how much progress he had made in making money and earning a reputation for himself. He was about to get even more famous.

Things were looking up. His slogan, "Better born lucky than rich" was proving to be true and he was on his way to the top.

Another postcard that Cosley sent to friends like J. J. West.
Picturc courtesy of Richard West.

Let's take a closer look at this country when Cosley first arrived.

CHAPTER 1

ARRIVAL IN MONTANA and CANADA'S NORTHWEST TERRITORIES (NWT)

Montana was made the 41st state in the union of United States of America. Her birthday was on November 8, 1889.

Some people said Joe Cosley traveled west to Montana arriving in time to see these celebrations in the mountain towns.

However, apparently he did not come out west to live in the cities or towns. Those close to Cosley understood he arrived in the mountain west to find wilderness areas where he could trap and hunt for all his needs. They state that Cosley was a mountain man who loved seclusion and the isolation and vastness of these towering Rockies.

Cosley had heard stories of the beautiful lakes and mountains and the abundance of game and furbearers and he wanted his share. He wanted to get away from civilization and be on his own. Joe told the fur buyer in Cardston he had heard as a kid that beaver taken from the headwaters of the Hudson Bay drainage system consistently brought higher prices. Now out west, he knew it was true.

Lots of individuals living back east wanted to head west and the call to "go west young man" moved Joe Cosley. He had dreamed of going west with free land, the shining mountains with an abundance of game and furbearers. Joe chose the rugged mountains of Northwest Montana. This virgin area was almost empty of civilization — just what young Joe wanted and needed.

We don't know all the reasons Joe went west, but we know he had wanted to go for some time.

Joe Cosley arrived in Montana during the late 1880's and hired on as a cowboy and cowpuncher. Some say Joe arrived in Montana in 1889.[3]

Frank Goble states that "The oldest two Cosley Trees in which Joe carved his name were dated 1887, located in Kishenehn Valley."[4]

According to his family, Joe left home in Ontario at age 17, sometime during 1886. Soon after his arrival in Montana, Glacier and Waterton became Joe Cosley Country.

The Causley Family

Marie Oketa was born July 31, 1845 to Marie Chawenakwetokwe Oketa. We do not have any information on her father other than his last name. Stephen Etienne Causley was born in 1836 in Goderich, Ontario.

They were married on February 17, 1863 in Goderich. There are ten children listed on the 1881 Canadian Census: Solomon, Andrew, Melissa A, Jane, Joseph, Mercilene, Heredetta, William, Margaret and Agnes. Daniel was born on October 1, 1881, after the census was taken.

This census shows that Joseph Clarence Causley was born in 1869 in Ontario, Canada, with the date confirmed by his family. Most published records say his father was a French Canadian trapper and his mother was Ojibwa.

Julia Nelson, who knew Joe personally as well as corresponding with Cosley's sister in Sault St. Marie, Ontario, states that Joe was one of twelve children. Their father, "a Frenchman, Stephen Causley," homesteaded at Blind River, Ontario. We do not fully understand Stephen Causley's ancestry, but Joe alluded that his father was of Spanish royalty. He drowned in 1882, four years before Joe left home.

Joe's Mother, Marie Oketa Causley spoke French, English and Chippewa-Cree. Stephen taught the children how to fish, trap and the backcountry ways, while Marie taught them language and refinements.

Joe attended the Shingwauk Indian Residential School in Sault Ste Marie, Ontario, 1877 to 1880 (age 8 to 11). Joe was known as Sahgahnuhquudoo: "Cloud Appearing". Blacksmith was his trade. Joe used these skills to build and repair traps, all of his life. While this is the only school record we have, Joe Cosley was obviously educated and a talented writer.

After W.W.I, Joe returned home to visit his mother. This was the last time that Joe saw his mother. She died on May 5, 1925 in Blind River, Ontario.

---

[3]Cosley told Joe Heimes that he arrived in Montana during the summer of 1889.

[4] Goble states that Ted Christiansen, son of former Waterton Park Warden R. M. Christiansen, has a section of an Aspen trunk with Joe's name and date 1887.

"Joe had a negative self-image as a Metis," said Jack Holterman. He further concluded that Joe attempted to compensate for it by his dress and life-style. Julia Nelson stated that when Joe came west he was called an Indian by every newspaper that covered his explorations. She concludes that they were all guessing, "for Joe told no one he was an Indian and hotly resented being called one."[5]

And yet, before, during and after the war, John Orville Bates said Joe referred to himself as an Indian. He even used a war-cry to signal. To Bates, an early homesteader kid in the Cardston area, Joe was a half breed Indian. To others, Joe did not want to be known as an Indian and he gave the impression he was not an Indian.

As proof to others that he was not an Indian, Joe, in his mid-life, grew a mustache and a goatee. It had a double advantage: Indians do not have facial hair and Joe's mustache and goatee made him look even more like Kootenay Brown, perhaps a role model.

Jerome (Jerry) DeSanto, the ranger in Belly River in 1966, wrote a great and detailed article[6] on Joe Cosely and Belly River. DeSanto quotes George Baker saying that Joe Cosley had, "enough Indian blood to make him love to go on the silent trails alone." That is probably the best way to describe the situation.

By the time Joe Cosley arrived out west, he could fancy shoot, fancy ride, tell fancy stories, and write beautiful poetry.

Arrival in Canada's Northwest Territories, now known as Alberta

Joe Cosley wrote several stories of his experiences in the mountains he so loved. One account was how Cosley came to meet John George Brown. Cosley was impressed with Brown from the very first, and wrote of him, "He was a small man, agile in movement and quick eyed. A Stetson buckskin sombrero crowned his head . . a bright red rose and a few green leaves painted on the under right-side of the brim. He wore a voyageur's sash, long fringed, hanging loosely at his side; a broad brocaded silk muffler about his neck, cowboy style. He had long hair that fell gracefully in wavelets over his shoulders. A gray mustache, terminating in points and slightly curved upward. He had the appearance of a typical frontiersman."[7]

---

[5] Julia Nelson, *"Cosley, Trapper and Guide Extraordinary"* Canadian Cattlemen Magazine, August, 1953

[6] Jerry DeSanto, *50 years in Glacier's back country . . . the legendary Joe Cosley*, Montana The Magazine of Western History, Winter, 1980 pages 12-27.

[7] Joseph Cosley, *The Meeting Of Kootenai (sic) Brown*, Joe may have been describing himself rather than Brown.

Brown talked with fancy descriptions of the mountains and the mountain way of life. He wore a uniform and badge and was paid to keep the peace in the park and to watch over the wildlife. Cosley liked Brown's style and flare and patterned some of his life after Kootenay. Cosley saw benefits that John George Brown had. After Kootenay Brown died, Cosley started saying that it was Brown who copied Cosley's dress and fancy way of speaking. No matter how you look at it, both men were unique and picturesque.

People who knew Cosley said Joe spoke "with choice diction and pleasing pronunciation," said John Bates. "And he wrote that way with rhythmic tones. He could describe something quite vividly and used the proper words to make it interesting," stated Bates.[8]

Cosley wrote extensively and sent articles to publications which printed them, gave him credit and paid him money. People in Northern Montana and Southern Alberta, including Bates, said how great his stories were.

John Bates had, "a number of articles by Joe Cosley describing his experiences on a trap line up in northern Canada. I learned later, that Cosley hadn't been up there yet, and he was in the park (Glacier) doing his trapping there and writing his experiences from the park. And it would be like Joe to do this," concluded Bates.[9]

Did Joe Cosley exaggerate to make a good story better? Yes. Watty Foster[10] said that Cosley, "liked to tell stories and he bragged. The stories and bragging seemed to increase to meet the situation." Bates conceded that Joe wasn't even up north, he was down south in Belly River when he wrote about his trapping experiences for the articles. "He wasn't even there! He was picturing what could have been," remarked Bates.

Virgin Territory

Joe Cosley liked the idea that Alberta was not yet a province and that the Northwest Territories were administered from Ottawa, Ontario, over 3,000 miles away. That was a long way from headquarters.

Cosley wrote of the wildlife up at Waterton[11], "A hot breath of chinook now swept gently over the land, bringing into existence many little streams from melting snow. The condition of the weather appeared

---

[8] John Orville Bates, interview taped by Paula Eid. Dustin, May 15, 1975, in connection with Glacier's Bicentennial Project of historical interviews.

[9] Bates, *op. cit.*

[10] Interview with the author while picking rock for a fireplace in Waterton.

[11] Joe Cosley, *The Meeting of Kootenai Brown*, p. 8

to have reverted to a state of kindliness, yet the sky showed not it's blue, but gave promise for the following day."

"In the folds of profound silence I sat, enjoying the warmth of the lazy air. After a time I arose, took my rifle and strolled out of the camp. There was a slight odor of perfume from exposed buttercups, which were badly crushed, but yet seemed to live for a purpose, I suppose to linger awhile to exude from their hearts sweet odor and waft it, with other dying blossoms, on the air."

It is reported that Joe Cosley drew this mural (and variations of this) on the home walls of different friends of his in Southern Alberta.
Picture courtesy of Richard West

"I wandered to the open flat whereon so many homes have since been erected, the pleasant sight of handsome structures created by mankind. This day, however, nothing of the sort greeted my eyes, save the great beauty of nature adorning the peaceful glades, the silent flat with it's verdant timbers unmarred by axe, and the splendid shore lines on which the cold water rise and fell so lightly in their wash. When the sun topped the jagged peaks to the west at eventide, elk, moose and deer came down from the pine forests which look like a velvet mantle on the uplands and drank the clear waters and rested on the green grassy flats around, for this place was far from the leather-scented trails of man."

Yes, Joe Cosley was a fine writer and over the years would be much acclaimed.

Lloyd "Bud" Spencer[12] of Lethbridge, Alberta feels that Montana was Joe's second love — his first being the land that would one day become Alberta, Canada. Bud writes in an unpublished work about his "Friend Joe" and I quote Bud,

"Joe called Canada a beautiful young land pregnant with opportunity," and that it was then and still is today.

"Alberta, born in 1905, (Alberta was founded in 1905) daughter of the Northwest Territories, adopted Joe. He (Joe) was tall, dark and handsome; as agile as the mountain lion and with eyes twinkling with the freedom of a mountain stream."

Bud knew the old timers in Mountain View, Beazer,[13] Boundary Creek,[14] and Waterton[15] who knew Cosley. Some of these people were Bud's relatives. Besides a collection of stories about Joe Cosley, Bud also has some pictures of Joe's drawings and carvings.

"I also have a picture of the tree where the $1,000.00 ring[16] is hidden in Alberta — the name and date, the (carving of) the hearts pierced with an arrow. It is a treasured possession," said Bud.

---

[12] L. "Bud" Spencer's letter to the author dated October 3, 1992 from his home in Lethbridge, Alberta.

[13] Beazer (hamlet) 49° 07'N 113° 29'W. The area's first homesteader, Mark Beazer, was the area's first postmaster and Mormon Bishop. Bought the homestead on this site in 1890.

[14] Boundary Creek (former locality) 49° 00'N 113° 22'W. It's small.

[15] Waterton Townsite 49° 3'N 113° 50'W. Lieutenant Blakiston named the lakes after Charles Waterton, an English naturalist who never saw his name-sake.

[16] Julia Nelson and Jerry DeSanto list this hidden ring as worth $1,500. It is not likely Cosley would ever purchase such a ring because of the cost. And certainly, no girl or women in Southern Alberta or Northern Montana would ever wear such a large ring. DeBeers, the world diamond authorities and suppliers, said a $1,000 or $1,500 diamond ring back in 1913 could be ½ to ¾ inch in diameter. Modest women in these parts would be embarrassed to wear such a large diamond. These were tough times and a diamond that big and valuable would buy a working ranch with buildings, water rights, cattle and horses.

CHAPTER 2

WATERTON PARK

Waterton Lakes National Park was originally established as a small "Forested Park" by an order in council in 1895. It was a 54 square mile mountainous area and a bold beginning to preserve our wilderness areas.

It was re-established as a Dominion Forest Reserve in 1906 called the Kootenay Forest Reserve and was subsequently made a "Dominion" Park in 1911. It became a National Park officially in 1930 with the tabling of the first National Park Act. Waterton was called Kootenay Lakes for a while before the name Waterton took hold.

In 1911 the park area was reduced to 13.5 square miles, then enlarged in 1914 to 423 square miles, but this is probably an under-estimation, says Rob Watt.[17] "The area was reduced in 1921 to 220 sq. miles and there have been a few boundary adjustments since that time. The official size today is 203 sq. miles."

One of the most colorful characters in western Canada was John George Brown. Brown was born October 10, 1839 in Ireland. He served briefly as an officer with the British Army in India, cir. 1858-1859. He resigned his commission and emigrated to Victoria, Canada in 1860 by boat, via the Panama Canal, with a brief stopover in California.

J. G. Brown worked around the goldfields of British Columbia's interior. He was Police Constable at Wildhorse Creek and a prison guard at New Westminister. Then he traveled to Fort Gary, Manitoba, and was there for several years.

He returned in 1873 where he was involved with the U.S. 1873/1874 International Boundary Survey Party, probably as a sutler or

[17] Rob Watt, Senior Park Warden with Parks Canada in Waterton Lakes.

camp cook or a civilian provisioner to the camp and occasional scout. He then remained in Fort Benton area, probably as a wolfer.

Brown then settled in the Waterton area and sold whiskey there. He started guiding visitors to the lakes and mountain with some success. His first wife died and J.G. married a full blood Cree woman by the name of "Blue Flash of Lightening" and he built a homestead. Early on Brown was appointed to the position of Fisheries Officer. Then he became the Forest Ranger

John Orville Bates remembers Kootenay Brown. "I remember his fish traps that he had in the river," states Bates. "I remember my dad telling me that it was illegal, but that *nobody* bothered Kootenay Brown."

John Bates went to the lakes with his family during the summer months. "We'd go up and stay a week, two weeks, ten days, and that's how I met Kootenay Brown at his cabin in Waterton. We would go up there and stay for a week or two and never see another soul, except Brown and later some other ranger would come by. There was never another soul in there. And that's why I don't like to go back there. It's spoiled now with the town. We caught all the fish we wanted."

Kootenay Brown Overseer [18]

Brown was involved with the establishment of the park. His influence started the ball rolling, with the original designation of the Waterton area as a "Forested Park." There is some indication that he helped rancher F.H. Godsal with the lobbying effort. He became directly involved in the future of the park in June of 1905 when he wrote a letter to his M.P. expressing concern regarding the future of the Waterton Forest Park Reserve.[19]

Again on August 6, 1909, J. G. Brown wrote to the Member of Parliament Herron regarding the state of what was then the Kootenai Forest Reserve:

> A park overseer is required. There have been over 500 people, picnic and tourists, here this season, a great number are here now. Many of them wantonly or thoughtlessly destroy shade trees and leave camp fires burning which are a menace to all of us, the mountains and all things. If I can obtain this office I am

---

[18] Goble states that Kootenay Brown's first homestead fronted on the Dardanelles River between the middle and lower lake; it included Pass Creek Flats.

[19] See Rodney, W. *Kootenai Brown: His Life and Times* 1836-1916, Sidney, B. C. : Gray's Publishing Ltd. 1969

willing to put up an office close to the lake and look after things to the best of my ability.

In February of 1910, under an order-in-council, special regulations were put in place by Ottawa for the "Kootenay" or Waterton Lakes Reserve which authorized the appointment of the areas first "game guardian."

Brown had lobbied for this position and was ultimately rewarded with the job.

John George (Kootenay) Brown is the second from right on the front row. His wife, Blue Flash of Lightening, is on the right in the back row near the door way. This is the new Park Office built near the lake. Celebrating this event were the local dignitaries and the Member of Parliament.
Picture courtesy of Glenbow Archives, Calgary, Alberta.

Over time John George Brown became known as "Kootenay" Brown for the following reasons:

1. He sold whisky to the Kootenay Indians on the west of the divide;
2. He lived next to the Kootenay Lakes (Waterton);
3. He wrote and initiated newspaper articles about Kootenay Lakes, his job there, and what visitors would find in the Park;
4. He campaigned for better jobs with the Government of Canada.

The parks people wrote the following report of Brown's passing: John George Brown, more commonly known as "Kootenay" Brown, died on July 18, 1916, after a short illness, at his home in the park. He was the first ranger in charge of the park, and, in fact, the existence of the park is largely due to his efforts to have protection afforded the game, as he realized that with the numbers of settlers in the country its destruction was certain," wrote Park Superintendent Cooper in his annual report.

Chief Superintendent Of Dominion Parks (P. C. Bernard-Harvey) also noted the following:

The Forest Ranger, John George Brown, better known in the neighborhood as Kootenay Brown, who was in charge of this park for several years, died in August, 1916 (sic), at an advanced age, and was buried at the site selected by himself overlooking the lower lake. He had lived in the locality for forty years and was the best known pioneer in the district.

Historian Ian Getty stated, "none of the accounts of Browns life are entirely reliable"[20] and should be approached with caution. Many of the popular accounts of Brown and his activities are clearly fictitious.

Brown was well known and admired by a large group of pioneers. Joe Cosley liked Brown for his "exceptionally good qualities" and his "wonderful education, as a student of scholastic excellence had no parallel."

Cosley also liked the way Brown was paid for publicizing Waterton and himself. Brown also got pay for looking after the wilderness, and he could still personally harvest game for himself.

Brown was not only a special friend of Joe Cosley — so was Blue Flash of Lightening. She was a full blood Cree[21] and she spoke Cosley's language.

Brown was a character and was influential in establishing Waterton as a park, preserved for the future.

---

[20] Perhaps this includes Cosley. In the article that the Albertan published on Cosley he states that he was a former scout with a regiment of U. S. cavalry under General Wilson A. Miles, who directed his troops against Sitting Bull. (see the end of Chapter 8). One of Brown's stories places him there also, "At one point, Brown was captured by Sitting Bull and a band of Sioux. . ." Waterton Lakes National Park by Heather Pringle, p. 68.

[21] Rob A. Watt, Attachment prepared on John George Brown, 21 Feb. 1998.

CHAPTER 3

PRE-PARK DAYS

Landmark changes were being made in the west. In 1895 the topography east of the continental divide, which had been allotted as a hunting ground for both the Blackfeet and Kootenais by the treaty of 1855, was purchased from the Indians for $1,500,000. This was the traditional account.

However, the government acquisition of this land was not a cash deal. The word "bought" is a myth and is a subject usually avoided, states Jack Holterman. "The deal was a lease which, according to Grinnell, might 'expire' and was conditional on the government making allotments, a condition that the government soon violated."

Other infractions included building the Hotel at East Glacier on the Blackfeet Reserve without even an attempt at striking a deal for the land. It was just a land grab.

Some mining had commenced in search for the mother lode but all these prospecting adventures were illegal before this purchase. However, after the purchase of this land it was legally opened to mining.

Rumors were rampant that this whole area would soon become a national park and all mining would be prohibited. Sharp-eyed prospectors abounded. Gold was discovered in the Black Hills of the Dakotas and surely there would be finds in Northwest Montana too. And there were, but not for long. The short mining boom period soon played out and all that was left behind were open mines, abandoned equipment, and place names throughout the area.

Joe Cosley in uniform. There is a log cabin being built behind him.
Picture courtesy of Glacier National Park

National Forests

By 1900, the National Forests were being established in Montana. These were the early days and there were many changes. The headquarters location for this area was in Belton.

It wasn't until 1905 that the forest service was fully organized and operating. The raises in pay were small but the notoriety of being a forest service ranger was increasing. Joe Cosley was hired as ranger for the Forest Service. He knew the area like the back of his hand. He said he had helped build Ahern Pass in the early days. It was common knowledge that Joe also trapped some of the area before the Forest Service.

Some rangers found they could earn extra money guiding for hire. Others, in the deep woods, never saw people, so there were no customers to guide.

Hunting was a different matter. Most towns and cities around the forest service had hunters who wanted to bag a trophy animal. They started asking these rangers where they should go to get the best that year. John Bates tells that his father, "used to go sheep hunting and they'd come home and tell how Joe Cosley had told them where to go to get the sheep." Other hunters talked about great hunting trips and Joe soon had the reputation of knowing where big game were; his expert help made hunting a lot easier and more rewarding.

New Belly River Station

Cosley was able to get a new ranger station built at Belly River in 1908 or 1909. This was the old old station. Besides a dwelling for the ranger, every ranger station had to have an outhouse, barn, coral and a flag pole. Things were looking up for Joe.

Daily Fare

What was it like in the days of the Forest Service? Trapping and hunting were allowed and in many areas almost expected. Forest Rangers were not paid very much so they had to earn extra money somewhere. Also, the over population of beaver or big game created problems. The rangers were expected to control beaver dams, and they could harvest deer or elk for their own needs.

The rule was, "surely a ranger was entitled to meat at any time."

In Montana's earlier days, the rangers were allowed to trap to supplement their income. It may not have been that much different in the early days before Alberta was made a province.

"Bert Barns stationed at the Canadian Belly River station," stated Frank Goble, "was trapping the Canadian side of the Belly River."

Barnes was there from the late 1920's to the mid-1930's when he was moved to Pass Creek station. Goble has direct knowledge of Barnes' success. "The fur buyer in Lethbridge told Levi Ashman, with whom I was trapping in the Akamina-Kishenina Valley, that 'that little guy from Waterton with the Cockney accent (meaning Bert Barns), brings in more fur than you do!'"

These were very different days from what we now have in parks. What was approved of back then is illegal now.

Making Friends and Visits

Joe Cosley made lots of friends, solid relationships that would remain as friendships forever. Chances are if Cosley stopped in to visit a rancher, he would be invited for supper. In turn, Cosley would share several of his exciting stories of recent adventures exploring the mountain west or a tale of his growing up years. "Your Joe" shared stories of exploring. You would know of his love for his way of life and the adventure it brought.

Cosley still visited his friends on both side of the border as if there were no border there at all. In those early days, one could travel in the mountains for weeks without ever seeing another human. There was no real border and people back then did not check into another country like we do today.

If Cosley frequented your home or your parent's ranch, probably you would have stopped what you were doing and welcomed him into your home. Then with Joe's exciting narratives, you wouldn't want the evening to ever end. These sagas were just for your ears and nobody else had ever heard those epics.

Each story had a real-life setting. His storytelling was unique yet universal. It touched a feeling in your life, no matter if you were old or young. Everyone understood Joe. You would say, "That is just the way it is sometime with me too."

Joe made people everywhere feel included in the situation. He painted the predicament in a way that it grabbed you and you were with him all the way to the very end. If Cosley had told your parents this story before, the story was now bigger with an improved ending.

"It was always a treat to see Joe coming to your place because that's when the excitement started.".[22]

---

[22] Over the years, (1953-1998) most people I have met who really knew Joe Cosley always talked of the privilege it was to be paid a visit by him.

CHAPTER 4

GLACIER NATIONAL PARK

Talk of the new national park had increased the last few years. The National Forest Rangers were told that they could apply to become Park Rangers but that someone else would be coming to do the hiring.

President Taft signed the bill creating Glacier National Park on May 11, 1910. Major W. R. Logan, the first Superintendent, was in Belton looking over applicants.

Joe Cosley was re-hired as a Park Ranger and assigned to the Belly River Station. Belly River, as far as the park was concerned, was Joe Cosley's. Some maps listed Belly River just as *Joe Cosley* because he was stationed there.

The Belly River Ranger Station was a prime pick for Joe. There was plenty of water, grass and wood and lots of game and furbearer.[23] The stream off Gable Mountain was cold enough that in the early years a "fridge" was maintained with this cool water running through it.

Cosley's former trapper's cabin was located down by the river, SW of the current station. He used this cabin starting in the late 1890's and

[23] Joe Cosley wasn't the only one trapping in the park when he was a Park Ranger. Frank Goble relates this: Many of the Park Rangers trapped and shot in the Park. The first Ranger at the head of Upper Waterton Lake invited Charlie Wise and Chance Beebe in to trap for the winter. They camped near the Little Kootenay Lakes, not far from the Ranger Station. Charlie told me: "There wuz lots of Marten dere, the Jeezely t'ings wuz all over d'place! D' Ranger would come an' visit us at our camp. We split d'take t'ree ways. Never hed Jeezely goog trappin'!"

even during the time when he was with the National Forest Service. He also had an additional cabin up at Cosley Lake.[24]

Joseph Clarence Cosley in new GNP uniform. See also Cosley's custom Stetson sombrero with bright red rose and a few green leaves painted on the right underside of the brim.

Glacier National Park

Earlier, Cosley would leave his station unlocked. But on August 7, 1910 Norton Pearl,[25] a new ranger to the park stopped in to see Cosley, the officer in charge of the Belly River Ranger Station. In the cabin down by the river Pearl found goat and deer hides hanging on the walls,

[24] Julia Nelson states there is a carving of J. C. Cosley dated 1897. This is believed to be located near Cosley's cabin at Cosley Lake.

[25] Leslie Lee, Backcountry Ranger in Glacier National Park, The diaries and photographs of Norton Pearl, Edited and Annotated by Leslie Lee.

traps, tea, and a bill on the table from H. S. Allen & Company Ltd. of Cardston, Alberta for $34.70 against William Webster.

However, when Pearl arrived at the new ranger station he found it to be locked up tight. He was unable to locate Cosley anywhere although he did find a quarter of venison hanging high from the barn. Cosley's favorite horses were in the pasture but no Cosley.

Cosley had several visitors from Glacier Park or should we say there were several that called at the Belly River Ranger Station to see Cosley. From talking to ranchers in Southern Alberta and Northern Montana near the park, Cosley always knew when others were in "his park." Cosley would stay out of sight and follow them to see what they were up to. If Cosley liked the visitor, he would host a fancy meal and gathering for him. If he didn't know the visitor, Cosley wasn't found.

Those familiar with Cosley, knew to signal him in some way like a whistle or bird sound. Those who didn't so signal, never seemed to see the elusive Joe Cosley in person.

On one leg around Glacier Park he trekked to Waterton. Colsey chose to leave after a full day of work and managed to arrive in time for the Saturday Night Dance. According to one of the stories Fred Burton printed in his newspaper, Cosley, "went on foot from the Polebridge Ranger Station to Waterton townsite (a distance of 30 miles) in 3½ hours. Lingering after the dance, he was still back at Polebridge long before breakfast and work."

A Winter Trip Around Glacier Park

Other rangers had been given the assignment to travel the perimeter of the park and report all events back to HQ. Back when the area was the Forest Service, both Ranger Albert Reynolds and Ranger Joe Cosley had been given this assignment. Old man Reynolds did very well but Cosley's circumnavigation was the fastest. However, it was also the least informative. Cosley just ran the distance and said he was finished when he returned back to home base.

Norton Pearl was also given this assignment in the winter months of 1913, and it was difficult. This year the snows were bad, the temperatures freezing, and the winds were awful. Beside all that, he didn't get much help from other rangers.

Pearl had never been to Waterton or west of there and he planned on stopping to talk to Cosley and have Joe show him the way to

Reynolds' two places.[26] Then the plan was to have Albert Reynolds show the way to Polebridge.

Things didn't go as planned.

Enroute Pearl had stopped at the snowshoe cabin at Slide Lake to see Cy Bellah, then he had planned to be off to Belly River and see Cosley. Cy needed some help, and one thing lead to another; over a week delay resulted.

On Friday, February 7, 1913, Norton and Cy finally snowshoed and hiked over Gable Pass and down to the Belly River Ranger Station. Cosley was not there. What they found was even worse. Let me quote from Pearl.[27]

> This is a hell of a place. Yes I said we were at Cosley's. Got in here just before dark and the only good thing is the water. Its a dirty damn place. He did have enough wood cut for tonight. We raked every corner for grub and did find an unopened ham and piece of bacon. Made our supper on that and rice. . . . He has just a little sugar and now a damn lot less, no condensed milk, no butter, tea, nor coffee, every dish dirty and he never has swept the floor or even tried to do so. I always had a better place for my dog. No dish pan or pot or anything to cook with. To say its a hell of a place for a man to stay in is putting it mildly. I've had more than a dozen old cabins that I didn't expect to use more than twice fixed up a hundred time better. This man must be a kind of a limit. They say he doesn't stay here much but hell, if he were here only once a month seems he'd have it a hell of a lot better than this. The sleeping place is as bad if not worse.[28]

Going over Gable, Norton and Cy saw Cosley's tracks following theirs at the summit as well as around Lee Creek. Joe's seemed to have been following Pearl's tracks a previous time.

The next day Cy went back to Slide and Norton into Canada looking for a ranch or someone who could tell him where to go to get to Kootenay Brown's in Waterton. It was late at night when Norton saw the

---

[26] Albert Reynolds had two cabins in the area called Waterton. His first, called the Boundary Camp, was located on the west shore of Upper Waterton Lake and just south of the international boundary line, near Boundary Creek. The second cabin Reynolds called the Home Office. It was located five miles south of the current Goat Haunt Ranger Station.

[27] Leslie Lee, op. cit.

[28] Leslie Lee, op. cit.

light in Brown's window. Norton learned that Reynolds had been taken to the hospital where he later died.

In Pearl's official report he was much kinder to Cosley:

> At dark we arrived at the station of Ranger Joe Cosley but found no one home. Neither did we find much to eat, and nothing in the form of cow products. The larder did contain ham and rice and with these we filled the biggest pot we could find. The cabin might have been cleaner and the sleeping quarters were nothing to brag of.
>
> I was disappointed at missing Cosley for I had expected him to go with me to Waterton Lake. I had no map of the Canadian region through which I had to pass and no one from whom I could get information.

Perhaps some mountain men lived like Pearl describes here, however, Joe was known as a clean dresser.

It was one thing having the new Belly River station all locked up during the warm months but it was a different matter come winter when rangers were enroute to far reaches of the big park. It was vital there be a place to stop over and get out of the weather.

The Belly River District is 150 square miles. When you add the Slide Lake area to Belly River, as it was in the early years, Belly River was just about as large as Waterton Lakes National Park is today. Waterton would not prevent a warden access to a warden station in summer or winter. To deny access in winter, could be life threatening.

Crosley, By Any Other Name

Crosley was a popular name down east in the early 1900's. It still is today. The name Crosley was also a brand name of an AM radio set that was manufactured in the east, and mostly sold there.

Perhaps when Glacier Park sent the names of lakes to the map makers, the name Cosley was interpreted as Crosley. Once it was on the maps and a sign located at the lake, people called it Crosley. Even rangers working at Belly River would use the Crosley name or Causley and Crossley. Early rangers also called the Belly River area, "Joes" to let others know what they were talking about. (There was only one Joe's.)

Perhaps the main reason people didn't know how Joe's last name was spelt was his quiet voice. Some folks just don't ask a person to repeat what they just said even when it wasn't understood the first time.

It is very difficult for families who were raised around Crosley Lake and Washboard Falls for fifty years to suddenly start to call it Cosley and White Quiver Falls. It wasn't until the late 1950's that the cartographers in Washington, D. C. got it right with the Cosley name.

More murals painted on a ranch or home wall of a Cosley friend.
Notice the alligator fancy saddle.
Picture courtesy of Richard West.

Place Names

Geographical localities get named by people who make the names stick, not necessarily the first to name the area or location.

Romanticist to the core, chivalrous Joe not only named mountains and lakes after his lady friends, he also wrote them poetry.

Joe Cosley named some of the lakes and mountains in Belly River. He actually started naming places prior to when he was in the Forest Service. Cosley apparently told more than one person he named a lake after them and to this day, there are several families who honestly believe Cosley was special to their great grandmother who passed the experience down.

Elizabeth Lake : Named for Joe's special love, Elizabeth Webster, who was born and raised in Mountain View, Alberta. Naming lakes after women he knew was just one way he became known as a "Ladies Man."

Max Pitcher of Cardston said Cosley named Elizabeth Lake after his mother, Elizabeth Hendry Pitcher. Her full maiden name was Jane Elizabeth Hendry and she told her family that Cosley originally name this lake Jane back in the late 1890's but when that name didn't hold, he went with Elizabeth.

Each Elizabeth felt special having a lake named after them by the famous trapper and mountain man, Joe Cosley. There are more.

Cosley told others in Montana that he named this lake after a daughter of Teddy Roosevelt. Cosley was the guide that took his two daughters through Belly River via Ahern. But, alas, Roosevelt's daughters were named Ethel and Alice.

Helen Lake : Cosley told two women that he named this lake after them. We don't know their names but Joe said[29] that both were a little cooler than Elizabeth. Cosley Trees with H. C. carved along with Cosley's name or initials have been seen.

In fact, it was Major Malcolm Clarke, an early surveyor, that named this after his daughter Helen P. Clarke. Helen and her sister ranched in Midvale not far from the Glacier Park Hotel.

Margaret Lake : Named this lake after his life-long friend,

Sue Lake : Cosley named this lake after Sue Henkel, an Indian girl near Babb, Montana. Joe frequented the Hinkels at Main.

Cosley Lake [30] Joe named this lake after himself and he had a cabin next to this lake. He told ranchers, in his usual elegant way, that this lake ran endlessly deep just like he did and there was no way anyone could fathom its lavish wonders.

Finally, it is called after its name-sake the way it should be spelled.

The "place names" Cosley got to stick, were by guiding tourists and government people throughout his Belly River. He would also tell them

[29] Interview with the author, Joe Heimes said that Cosley told him that the Helen person that Cosley said he named that lake after was a little cool. Heimes didn't know what to believe.

[30] Joe Heimes told the author he was glad the Washington boys finally got it right naming Crosley or Crossley as Cosley. Heimes felt it should be called Cosley because that was his name and that's how Cosley spelt his name.

the names of plants and flowers and the botanical name as well. Cosley was the unacknowledged first ranger naturalist of Glacier / Waterton.[31]

Bertha Lake : The older name for this lake is Spirit Lake. Joe claimed he named this lake for a lady friend of his, but we don't know who. The name that stuck is attributed to a homesteader in Waterton village.[32]

Cosley Country

He explored more than just Belly River for near 40 years and knew the area like no other. Cosley had a long international list of close friends he visited, and he kept in contact with each of them. His special friends were Kootenay Brown and Blue Flash of Lightening, George Hinkel in Babb, the Howes of Lake McDonald, DeLance Strate of Waterton, the Wests and Websters of Mountain View, the list goes on.

Joe continued to enjoy a social life as a charming and courteous guest to the ranchers along the border. He left a trail of trees marked with his carved initials and a few with hearts pierced with arrows around his initials.

Cosley was elusive. He could travel any part of Glacier or Waterton and not be detected. He prided himself on that; perhaps it was his Indian heritage. A person only ran into Cosley if Cosley wanted him to. He prided himself on that ability.

Cosley regularly traversed between Columbia Falls and Mountain View via Belton, Ahern Pass and Belly River. Early on he built a cabin on the Canadian side and 8 miles south of that was another near the confluence of the south and middle fork of the Belly River.

Norton Pearl said of Joe's haunt, "Some of the best photographs I have ever seen of the park. Many of these were taken in the grandly scenic and little known Belly River country."

Belly River soon became known as the best district to be over because it was so beautiful and so far from Head Quarters. The best of the best in every way.

Belly River became known as Cosley Country, Land of Legends.

---

[31] Jack Holterman, Place Names of Glacier / Waterton Parks,

[32] Jack Holterman, Op. Cit.

CHAPTER 5

JOE COSLEY, THE LEGEND

Joe Cosley was tall and good-looking with distinctively Indian features. He wore a red voyageur's sash and gold rings adorned his ears. He became an expert trapper and sold his furs to buy fancy clothes, gear, saddles and to outfit his horse. In short, Joe was eventually a sort of a hippie mountain man.

There seems to be two or more Joe Cosley's. There is the Cosley that most people in Southern Alberta and Northern Montana have heard about, and they adore him.

Then there is another, though smaller, group that have heard about Cosley, and they just don't think it is all true. Some old timers personally knew Cosley and did not want him anywhere near[33] their daughter or sister or even themselves.

Will the real Joseph Clarence Cosley please stand up?

For a long time, I too was in the first group. Yes, I was a legend lover of everything that Joe Cosley ever did, including things that were just said about him. I felt he was a very fascinating person that made his mark on Glacier and Waterton and the surrounding communities in Montana and Alberta. No matter what we believe today, Cosley has become a part of us.

Probably the truth of any situation is somewhere in-between these two extremes. Over the next chapters, we will attempt to bring out original "facts" as well as additional information.

Let's look at some of the ways Cosley left his mark in Glacier and Waterton Parks and on us.

---

[33] Lloyd "Bud" Spencer, in conversation with author, said that one family head, by the name of Webster was adamant about Cosley not seeing any of his girls.

Cosley Trees

It seems that everywhere Joe Cosley went and worked, he left his mark on the territory. Just like any wild thing that marks its highlands, Joe staked his turf and marked his terrain by carving his name or his initials in trees. Over the lifetime of Joe Cosley, you would find hundred and hundreds of "Cosley Trees" with his name engraved so well that the tree would not scar-over the carving. It was a Cosley tradition.

Cosley Tree, dated June 2 / 08. Picture courtesy of Owen McClung

If you want to learn how Cosley was so good at tree carving that out lasted a century,[34] try practicing on a banana with a ball-point pen. Let time be your partner and not brute force.

---

[34] Julia Nelson in, "Cosley, Trapper and Guide Extraordinary" Canadian Cattlemen, part two, September, 1953 states that there are tree carvings with the date as early as 1897 in the Belly River area.

Thousands of people know about Cosley Trees just like they do Cosley Stories and Cosley Trails.

Joe Cosley, Nov 09, 1897. More on this historic find in Appendices
Photo taken by Edwin Knox, on November 9, 1997

However, as plentiful as Cosley Trees were, they were also hard to find. Many hikers would never even spot a Cosley carved tree while companion hikers did.

Cosley Trees are also tied to Joe's romantic side. Joe would carve his initials above or below the one he loved. Some of these also had hearts around the initials and an arrow going through the heart. There are Cosley Trees still standing today.

Joe Cosley's artist talents were not limited to engraving trees. He sketched pictures, wrote articles and told stories.

Joe often sent friends a letter. John Bates recalls his father, "getting a letter from Joe but it was not in writing, but in pictures. Joe was "quite a cartoonist," said Bates. In this "letter" Bates remembered that, "Joe pictured himself with a broken toe and he showed how he broke his toe, then walking around with it bandaged up. I can remember my father showing around this letter in pictures to different people."

People Close To Joe Cosley

In order to see the big picture of Cosley, we must see who the players were in Joe's life. From the time he arrived in Northern Montana and in what was to become Southern Alberta, Cosley made lots of friends both in Montana and in Canada. These friends remained friends for life. Cosley was a very clean, nice-looking well-built young man. He was very polite, old-fashioned politeness, tipping his hat to the ladies.[35]

To the ladies, Joe was a ladies man. He wrote them poetry, named lakes after some, stopped by for lengthy visits and told colorful stories of the wilderness. Over the years he sent letters or came to visit again. He was always writing poetry to someone for their special occasions.

Yet to the men Joe was a man's man. He was a trapper, adventurer, and soldier who told of experiencing hardship and violence and valor. Cosley was a hero on all fronts.

Kids adored Joe and his special stories just for them or a carved animal gift. Elizabeth remembered when she was 8 or 9 and Cosley stayed in Cardston with the Hendry family some winters. He would tell her stories of the mountains while she sat on his lap. To Jane Elizabeth, Joe was hers and only hers. He drew pictures of animals for others.

To the public, Joe was also a famous mountain man explorer who traveled the west and the world. He was the David who won over the giant Goliath government.

If your family experienced a visit from Joe Cosley you may well feel it was a privilege. Cosley knew and visited ranch families all over the foothills and mountains of Southern Alberta. Names like West, Webster, Sanders, Nelson, Strate, Archibald, Foster, Beazer, Bevans, Beebe, Brown, Caldwell, Hansen, Wright, Okey, Welsh, Neville, Haslame, Allen, Jensen, Haug, Nixon, Jessop, Chipps, Jenkins, Blackmore, Woolf, Lehr, Earl, Parrish, Pilling, Scott, Cooper, Jacobs, Ivins, McKeaque, Shattuck, Simpson, Selby, Arndt, Thompson, Leavitt, Ehlert, Broadhead, Walburger, Findlay, Watson, Kearl, Vais, Workman, Moir, Henderson, Burnside, Payne, Burrows, Tolly, Fiddler, Vadnais, Bates, Martin, Pyle, Allred, Tolley, Davis, Wynder, Ehlert, Peterson, Olsen, Prince, Jessop, Zuebeck, Davidson, and a whole lot more than I can remember. Other families have moved away from their rural roots; however, Cosley knew them.

Secrets Kept Is Love Untold

One such person that was touched by the magic of Joe Cosley was Lloyd "Bud" Spencer, now living in Lethbridge, Alberta. He remembers when he first heard about Joe Cosley and then actually met him over the years. Bud is glad he kept a diary and that it has helped him to remember all he was told.

---

[35] Dorothy Brading of Columbia Falls in conversation with the author

“Once when I needed a home I stayed with my Aunt Mae and Uncle Billy Webster in Mountain View,” recalls Bud. “Billy is Elizabeth Webster’s brother.”

“Billy took me for a ride up where the mountains touch the sky, where cool shadows creep, rest, and sleep, and the silent winds go by.

“I rode Billy’s pink pinto Cyoose. The only horse to out run that pony was Joe Cosley’s trusted old horse called, ‘Vassar.’

“Billy took me to the ‘Big Rock’ and we stopped and rested. He pointed out Mountain View, Caldwell, Hillspring, Twin Butte and Glenwood; the St. Mary, the Belly, the Waterton rivers, many lakes, Beaver Dam, Payne, Dipping Vat and others.

“Then we rode to a little lake. On the south side of this lake was a little round green meadow where Golden Lady Slippers grew. Billy said the blazes on the trees marked the Cosley Trail.

“When we returned home Aunt Mae asked me where we had been. I told her to the lake on the hill and the little meadow where the Lady Slippers grew. You know, Aunt Mae, those yellow flowers growing in that green meadow look just like a ring.”

“Billy,” asked Aunt Mae, “isn’t that the spot where Joe Cosley proposed to Elizabeth?” “Yes, replied Aunt Mae, but that’s Elizabeth’s secret.

PROPOSAL by Joe Cosley

There is love and beauty sublime
In thy form of grace divine;
A haven of eternal rest
In thy companionship so blest.
Wilt thou listen now
To my sacred vow!
My life I would give to thee
If thou would’st give thine to me.
Ah lovely maiden, kind and true,
Through these lines I appeal to you;
Pause, Oh pause along the path of life
Thou queen of loveliness, and become my wife.
Then thy love I’d fondly cherish,
Thy presence forever adore;
Neither should ever perish
But to blossom evermore

Continuing he writes, “Sometimes it took my ‘Friend Joe’ days to track down a marten. He ate what he caught.” We know he lived off the mountains.

Bud wrote a poem about Joe's love for Glacier, Waterton, and Alberta. He entitled the poem "The Rock" which was published in the Lethbridge newspaper.

The Rock

God made the earth, then He made me,
Turned me loose in His world to roam.
Gave me my choice of all His land,
In which to build my home.

There's a large white rock on a blue-green hill,
Right close to where I stood.
God sat on this rock and rested,
Looked on His work and said, "It's good."

A trail through the valley winds up through the pines,
To a place where secrets keep.
By a little lake nestled on a flowered hill,
Like a dimple in nature's cheek.

I circled the lake, on the southern shore
Runs a cold stream crystal clear.
A deer and her fawn watched while I drank,
And I felt that God was near.

I saw the moon enter the heaven,
I watched it light playgrounds that night,
I watched it play games with its children - the stars
I watched 'til it ducked out of sight.

The sun peeked over the hilltops,
While Mother Nature painted a scene.
The winds blew free from sea to sea,
In this land so fresh and clean.

Next morning I left the foothills,
Went to see if I could find.
Another spot in this clean new land,
As good as, I left behind.

I saw streams running over beds of ore,
As I traveled north to the Arctic Sea.
Found the pot-of-gold at the rainbow's end,
But the back trails beckoned me.

I traveled south where the desert mirage,
Lifts gently towards the sky.
The hills and lakes, its illusions made,
Then like dreams they fade and die.

Where east meets west, and north meets south,
I came back to Alberta to rest.
Like a homing dove, to the land that I love,
I've stayed 'cause I like it best.

Bud Spencer

When Joe Cosley left his homeland he first traveled to Southern Arizona but he didn't like it there. Then he wandered to the territory that would soon become Montana. It was the part of the northwest corner or what we call Glacier today that first attracted his heart. But his real love was the country to the north in Canada's Northwest Territories that years later would become the province of Alberta. It was the people.

Joe visited friends in Main, Columbia Falls, Belton, and Apgar. Charlie and Maggie Howe hailed from Wisconsin and belonged to the Chippewa tribe. With Joe Cosley, Mrs. Brewster, the Sansevere family and others, they formed a Chippewa-Cree community at Lake McDonald.[36] Charlie stored furs collected from Joe Cosley and other trappers, trading with Lewis at the head of the lake.

As much as it sounds like Joe spent most of his "days off" from trapping in Canada, it may be more accurate to say, that for Joe, home was where he was at the moment. To Joe, both areas were so interconnected. So even though the two federal governments wanted to divide the two countries by a fine line we call the border, Joe didn't.

Wildlife wander from side to side and still do today. To elk, deer, beaver, mink, otter and muskrat, there really is no boundary that can keep them on one side or the other. Animals wander up and down their habitat, not from one country to another.

Natives wandered at will to the mountains during the summer and the prairies for the winter. They followed the migrations of the elk and buffalo for logical reasons. It was white man that installed a perimeter or demarcation line to keep the two countries defined.

Belly River and its the surrounding mountains have special meaning to natives from both sides of the border.

Chief Mountain, a towering landmark that can be seen a hundred miles or more in three directions, has been used by Indians of many

---

[36] Jack Holterman, *Place Names of Glacier / Waterton Parks.*

tribes as a shrine and traditional Mecca for the vision quest since prehistoric times. Many Indians come here to pray and participate in the sweat lodge, returning often. Also called "Altar Mountain," it is on the Blackfeet Reserve and white tourists should respect this holy land.

Joe Cosley chose Belly River because it was in the mountains that he loved and it was connected to Southern Alberta and its people. That was the unit for him. From all the accounts that I have read I think Joe felt that mountains and animals were his life, and that man's recent law did not particularly pertain to him.

On July 2, 1992, an earthquake centered south of Browning was rated 4.6 on the Richter scale. Soon afterwards a great block of rock split off the North face of Chief Mountain, spreading havoc over 500 acres. It remains a "focal mountain" and locals measure the view (the angle of the mountain) they can see from their ranch or home as "their" Chief Mountain.
Photo courtesy of Owen McClung

According to Spencer, even when Cosley traveled to Northern Alberta and Northern Saskatchewan, he still liked Southern Alberta the best.

Wherever he roamed, Cosley Stories were sure to follow close behind.

CHAPTER 6

COSLEY STORIES

Stories that make people famous tend to have several common threads interwoven deep into each narrative that makes them legendary. Cosley Stories are no different. Each folk tale chronicles Cosley at his best or most human, weaving the fabric of Alberta and Montana history.

Life stories told, and hopefully preserved, give meaning to life. It is true personal experiences that focus our lives. Alas, when individual tales become bigger than what really happen, people see the difference between what was said and what was done.

Common Cosley Story Threads

1. The more each story was told the more detailed each became and the better Cosley's talents could be seen.
2. Joe Cosley was always the shining knight on the white horse that knew the tricks to get ahead.
3. Cosley stories became history and were published in both countries, in black and white, and established his rightful fame.
4. Cosley always took the high road and was a gentleman.
5. Nobody was going to get the last laugh on Joe.

Extensive Press Coverage

Joe Cosley apparently told different stories or versions of those stories on different sides of the border. It was apparently on a need-to-know basis. If Cosley needed you to know something so he could get something from you — he told you that version of the story that would accomplish his goal. The other principle is success begets success. When a story works one time, it is tried again with someone else.

There seemed to be more written in southern and central Alberta, perhaps because he spent his summers there. However, the real reason more was written about Joe Cosley in Alberta was those in the communities there was a local newspaper that would print just about anything to fill space. Much printed has not been preserved.

Typical Alberta Story of Joe Cosley [37]

Joe Cosley enjoyed telling stories of his experiences. Now, whether they were all his experiences or just stories made up is another matter. Based on accounts published in newspapers and augmented by Cosley in what he told others, the verbal version of the typical Joe Cosley story goes like this:

> *Joe was born wealthy into an Algonquin*[38] *Indian tribe and quickly distinguished himself as a leader. With his aristocratic birth, he was college educated and he lectured in many places on both sides of the border about wildlife and natural resources.*
>
> *He was an expert sharp/shooter, horseman and rode in Buffalo Bill's Wild West Show for several years. Coming out West, he fought a knife battle with a Sioux warrior and won. The fight lasted several hours and Cosley was stabbed several times but was victorious. However, it took Cosley over a year to recover from the knife wounds.*
>
> *He moved west as a young man to hunt and trap. As proof that Joe was the strongest and fastest in the mountains, "he could set out across trail less timbered wilderness and cover sixty miles a day on foot or on snowshoes."*
>
> *On Cosley's trapline in Alberta, just 2 miles north of the USA border a renegade Park Ranger from Montana arrested him just to make a name for the ranger. Cosley was hustled to trial where he explained to park officials what happened. When they checked out his story, Joe was released to go with their apologies. Cosley had the last laugh when the park punished the ranger by firing him.*
>
> *That evening, Joe Cosley snow shoed over Ahern Pass, through snow-packed mountains to retrieve his fur and traps. Then he went to one of his friends (Waddy Foster) in Waterton*

---

[37] Told around Cardston, Mountain View, Lethbridge, Waterton, and surrounding communities.

[38] His mother was Ottawa and Cosley spoke Cree and Chippewa. Ottawa and Cree and Chippewa are all Algonquin. Not all wealth is money. Certainly, heritage, even when others say you are penniless, is priceless.

townsite and bought a boat, loaded his furs and rowed down river to Medicine Hat where he took the train to Toronto to sell them for the best price he ever received. Then he booked passage to Paris. After touring France he bought a large diamond worth anywhere from $1,000 up to $1,500 (depending on the story). *Joe had it mounted on a ring.*

On his return to Mountain View he proposed marriage to his sweetheart. She said no because she would not marry out of her faith. A year later, still hurt that he was turned down and realizing he loved only her, he buried the diamond ring in a poplar tree in Belly River.

One story has it that to disguise this sacred tree he started carving his initials in nearby trees every chance he had. He said he carved J C Cosley and the date all on the north side of the tree pointing to his loved one back in Alberta. Some believe this ring is still there. He joined the Canadian Army as a sharpshooter and quickly became a war hero shooting more German soldiers than any other Canadian and was decorated. Joe was a sniper and he shot German snipers.

Over the years he tended his traplines in Northern Montana and Southern Alberta. He built six cabins, all near Mountain View, Alberta.

In his later life Joe trapped in Northern Saskatchewan and Alberta and kept a daily diary complete with drawings on his life and times.

Montana Version [39]

Cosley disappeared mysteriously from his Montana haunts. When the war was over he came back with a pocket full of medals from the British government. Cosley isn't given much to talk. So when his friends asked him where he had been, he just took out the medals and jingled them in his hand, saying, "I enlisted and went over with the Canadian forces as a sharpshooter. They checked up on my shooting and when the King found I had picked off 500 Germans in four years of sniping, he gave me these medals.

These figures are not an exaggeration as the Canadian war records will show. Montanans who know Cosley's

[39] Glacier National Park record. It looks like there is more that precedes this story and what we have today is page two of the article.

mountain record with the rifle did not have any reason to doubt his story.

Joe fell in love with an Indian girl on the Glacier National Park Reservation just before he went away to become a soldier, and he put a thousand dollar ring on her finger to seal the sacred secret. Later word came across the mountains to him that his fiancee was talking lightly of the incident. All the Indian came out in Joe instantly. He snowshoed 60 miles over the mountains to get back the ring from this girl who was making a laughing stock of him.

An acquaintance who was among the first to greet Joe on his return from war jokingly referred to the incident, whereupon Joe said, "Yes, I got the ring back all right, and cached it in a favorite friendly old tree on the shore of Cosley Lake the last thing before starting over the line to go to war. Tomorrow I will be back at the cabin and get it, for I need the money." It was there just where he left it, in a hole which he had augered in the trunk and afterward plugged with a round peg. Cosley Lake, where Joe lives, was named for him. He is 46 years of age, and it is said (he) has a little aristocratic Spanish blood in his veins.

There is no denying that Cosley loved Belly River.
Can you see the similarities?

As a kid growing up in Southern Alberta, I believed that Cosley was a hero in every way. I imagined this history would make a great Hollywood Western staring Gary Cooper as the famous Joe Cosley. As time rolled on, other stars had to be Clint Eastwood or Mel Gibson. It was my guess that Cosley would have agreed with my choices.

As I found out more about Cosley's trial and what time he left West Glacier to race the evil park rangers, I started to write a movie script that covered each mile of terrain. And in my enthusiasm, I spread this story to anyone who would listen, and those who would not got it anyway. I still think it a great story for Hollywood. Movies can be creative with the truth, and tell a great story that entertains.

Fred Burton[40] was in the newspaper business in Cardston from 1901 to 1964. During this period the name of the paper changed from

[40] Verena Crawford, Chief Mountain Country: A History of Cardston and District, 1978, Page 24-26.

Alberta Star, to The Globe, then Cardston Review and finally the Cardston News.

During the fall of 1957, after reading a newspaper article in the Lethbridge Herald about Joseph Cosley, I talked to publisher Burton about his experiences with Cosley. First of all, Fred Burton is a nice person. He is honest and understanding. He also had a great memory. Fred recalled stories about Joe Cosley that were printed in the Cardston newspaper for 25 years from 1905 to 1929. Cosley came to the newspaper in Cardston in 1905 when the Forest Service north of Kalispell was developing. Joe Cosley had been hired as a forest ranger and he mostly served in Belly River. Lots of people in or near Mountain View and Waterton knew Joe Cosley as a frequent visitor at their ranches for years.

I asked Fred Burton[41] if he had any copies of past stories in the paper on Joe Cosley. Recalling some of the early days Fred regretted that the best stories on Cosley were lost in a flood of Cardston in 1925. Old copies of the Alberta Star, Globe, Cardston Review and the Cardston News were damaged when the storage basement filled with water. The library didn't have room for newspapers and he stopped saving copies after that flood.

Even though decades had passed, Fred could still remember Joe and the stories he brought to the paper. Fred even served in the war with Joe.

Burton spoke in specifics as he retold of time long ago.

"Joe would always come to the newspaper with a story of adventure in the mountains," said Burton. The newspaper never went to Cosley. Then he talked about Cosley's quiet side. "Cosley never talked to me about his "love" with women," ended Burton.

I asked if he had heard about Cosley being turned down in marriage by a Mountain View girl? Fred answered, "A Cardston girl, a Mountain View girl, a woman in Waterton, one in Boundary Creek and one in Babb, Montana." Fred knew several of their names but he didn't want to discuss them with me. "Joe is dead now and so are those stories."

However, Fred did tell me that two older girls or young women did come in to the paper inquiring about what was needed to make an announcement in the Cardston paper. He said that none of them ever did bring in the actual announcement.

Burton said: "When Cosley first came to the newspaper he actually wanted the paper to give him money in exchange for his stories. But we were always just a small town paper and could never pay anybody that didn't work at the paper. There were times we had a hard time even

---

[41] Fred Burton, Publisher and Editor of the *Cardston News* et al.

paying our workers." Fred continued with this point. "There were many times the paper didn't have the money to pay either the staff or me, but somehow the paper would eventually catch up. I certainly wasn't going to pay Cosley, or anyone else, for the opportunity to interview them for their story." said Burton. He meant it.

Then Fred said he told Cosley that there was space in the paper where Cosley could advertise and Cosley could say anything he wanted to, but that Joe then wanted the stories told free.

After Joe's first attempt to get paid, he agreed that the story printed and circulated around town and the district would give him more "ballyhoo," than a story not printed.

"Cosley sought notoriety and got attention for himself. However it wasn't just one way. The paper got something back in the exchange -- local copy made the paper more famous.

"Cosley would state his story like this," began Burton. 'People who know me say I am a hard-riding, buckaroo, willing to fight to the death but I want to put all that behind me now and take life easier.' or 'He could set out across trailless timbered wilderness and cover sixty miles a day on foot or on snowshoes.' or 'Some say that I joined the army as a sharpshooter, but I don't want to brag.'"

Fred said that Cosley always talked that way and that's how he started each story he brought to the paper.

Fred told me he didn't print every story Joe wanted printed nor did Fred typeset Cosley's stories just the way Cosley told them. Fred always cut something out of a Cosley story and felt what he left in would be taken by readers as creative and entertaining.

CHAPTER 7

FIRE COSLEY

Before Joe Cosley was hired as a ranger in the National Forest Service, he had hunted large game and sold or traded to nearby rancher friends. Cosley had trapped the area since at least 1890. It wasn't just him. Everyone did it.

When Cosley was re-hired as one of the first rangers for Glacier National Park, it was no secret what he was doing.

In August of 1910, Major William R. Logan's choice for park rangers was hunters, trappers, and mountain men already familiar with the wilderness and how to take care of themselves. With Joe Cosley and some others, Logan employed the fundamental rule of thumb that "it takes a thief to catch a thief.[42] Cosley had presented gifts of furs to Charlie Howe and authorities in the park. Cosley also sold some of his pelts to Howe. The Park knew what Cosley had done and what he was currently doing when they hired him.

In the early years of the park, it was okay for rangers to shoot any game they needed. Eventually that changed. It was the trapping (and selling what you trapped) that was not allowed any more. Cosley and all the other rangers were told to be on the lookout for anyone who came into the park to trap or poach.

Cosley was actually caught trapping in the Park in 1911 and was fired.[43] However, the firing didn't seem to be final. Cosley returned to Belly River and continued as ranger there until the summer of 1914.

---

[42] Substitute, "trapper," or "poacher," or "robber," or "smuggler," or "trespasser."

[43] While stationed at Belly River Joe regularly traveled outside his district to other areas in the park. Perhaps he had been visiting in Apgar or Columbia Falls

The National Park System was still somewhat new. Updated regulations arrived periodically. Then it took time to get the word out to the far reaches of the backcountry mountain stations.

Summer would be the only time to get everyone together to explain new procedure and regulations.

I speculate that Cosley and the other rangers found out about the new "no trapping" during the meeting that was called the first few days of July, 1912. This was a year after Cosley had been "fired." Maybe that firing was changed to a warning for that one time, but the new regulation was even more clear and strict.

Glacier National Park Suspicions

Park officials suspected Joe Cosley had never stopped trapping and hunting or poaching in the Park. They heard stories that Joe continued selling pelts in both Cardston and Lethbridge. Joe Heimes said that over time these stories eventually found their way to Park headquarters. In addition to Cosley's fur sales there were confirmed accounts of Joe supplying elk and trophy animals directly from Belly River to anybody in Alberta or Montana who wanted big game and was willing to pay Joe for his trouble.

The park had to confirm whether or not the stories were true. Several were verified, but officials wanted concrete evidence. They sent rangers in to check up on him. Wardens on the Canadian side tried tracking him for years.[44] They all tried to catch Cosley in the act of poaching and trapping furs or at least to capture him inside their respective parks with the goods in his possession, but they never did. Not until Joe Heimes.

Not only could they not catch Cosley with the goods, they couldn't even locate him. They saw signs but not Joe. Cosley was too wily.

Eventually, trapping in the park was unacceptable. It didn't matter if the trapping was being done by someone from the outside of the park or within. It had to be stopped. Glacier could not catch Cosley in the act and they could not spare enough employees to be checking up on Joe all the time. The decision was made in May, 1914 that since they could not stop Joe from breaking the law or catch him in the act, the Park was not

---

or even to headquarters. Cosley had trapped all over the park and this time he was caught. He was near the confluence of the Middle Fork and North Fork of the Flathead and Ralph Thayer, acting on orders from the superintendent, fired Colsey. Thayer didn't have much use for Cosley before or afterwards.

[44] Jack Holterman, *"Let the Mountains Sing"*

going to continue to pay him and employ him as the Ranger for Belly River.

The Park decided to stop paying Cosley and to send someone from the Park into Belly River to find Cosley and give him notice to get out and never come back. Now the question was who to send to tell Joe Cosley he was fired for good.

Heimes stated that the Park asked different rangers to go and do the deed, but for various reasons there were no takers. Most just did not want to deal with Cosley in Cosley's Belly River Country.

Who could they send to do this job? In June the Park asked Ralph Thayer who apparently said one word. If you knew Ralph, one word was a lot. We don't know which way Ralph traveled into Belly River but is a lot closer to go by way of Ahern Pass. However, at that time of year the pass and the rock outcrops would be snow packed and icy. There is no record of him going into Canada to Mountain View and arranging for a horse from J. J. West's dad, but that is likely the way he went in.

All we really know is that Cosley left Belly River in a big hurry and he didn't want to see Ralph Thayer ever again or even to talk about Thayer.

Heimes said that Ralph Thayer found Cosley near his station cabin and told Joe to get out of the park and never come back. He told Joe his pay was cut off, and that he would never see another cent. He also left a personal message to Cosley: As a ranger in Glacier National Park, you were sworn to protect the wildlife in the park. Stories abound from both sides of the border that you are still selling fur and game outside the park. Thayer told Joe that he should be ashamed being a Ranger.

His parting shot was, "If I ever catch you on the trails in this park again, I will kill you." Without saying a word, Cosley left the Belly River valley for Canada immediately.

Thayer went to the station and found it dirty and messy beyond belief, Joe's dinner was hot on the stove and a plate on the table.

It looks like Cosley took Thayer's warning seriously and never returned to the ranger station, not even to pick-up personal items.

So Joe Cosley found he was out of work in early June. He probably didn't want to risk returning to Glacier National Park and being caught, especially not after the threat he had received.

Now there is evidence that Joe did return to get his personal items, and he also took his snowshoes and some other gear. But his pay check had been cut off and he was between jobs. Besides, his trapline had been poached back that season, and the following two seasons would yield small harvests of fur. I think Joe recognized this was the time to go somewhere else for a few years and let his haunt refurbish itself.

On June 28, 1914, an assassin gunned down Archduke Francis Ferdinand of Austria-Hungary in Sarajevo, the capital of Austria-Hungary's province of Bosnia-Herze-govina. This triggered the war.

Newspapers everywhere had headlines and stories about the event and the conditions leading up to this. And there were discussions regarding the different treaties between countries and who was going to take a stand. Joe Cosley was in Cardston and Mountain View at this time, and he would have learned of the situation in Europe. It was the talk of the town and all of Southern Alberta.

CHAPTER 8

THE WAR

Cosley is in the middle of second row. Taken in Calgary by W. Rins in 1915. (Back L-R): W. Leavitt, N. A. Sorsensen, P. Yarns, A. Sheffield, W. Bergstrom, W. Berryessa. (Fourth Row): G. Cahoon, A. E. Woodward, F. W. Burton, J. Clanney, A. Gibb, A. B. McClachlan. (Third Row): J. W. Roberts, R. Gold, H. Daines, C. F. Broadbent, S. Bohne, J. Holmes. (Second Row): N. Ramsey, A. Jensen, C. G. Barman, J. C. Cosley, W. Glover, R. G. Buist, W. Woodward. (Front): J. Brooks, L. M. Brown, A. Dower, B. H. May, H. J. Devenish, A. P. Lye, H. Broadbent.
Courtesy of Glenbow-Alberta Institute, Calgary, Alberta

World War I

The war to end all wars, World War I, started July 28, 1914. A few days later Canada joined with England in declaring war on its enemies.

Joe's luck was with him. What better timing for a major event to come along than a war where he could prove his manhood to others and to be somewhere else. It was a winning decision for the young tiger Joe. Now Joe could tell his friends that he quit the park for good reason.

Historically, furriers and trappers have stated that in 1914 the fur harvest was high. In 1914 Hudson's Bay Company reported that they marked 37,553 beaver, 851,156 muskrats, 487 silver fox and 14,960 lynx. The war had a severe impact on the fur market. In 1915 the totals were 10,690 beaver, 127,087 muskrats, 251 silver fox, 6,508 lynx. Trapping markets were one of the casualties of the war.

Joe Cosley in his new Canadian Army uniform.
Picture courtesy of Richard West.

Cosley volunteered to serve in the Canadian Over-Seas Expeditionary Force on February 4, 1915. Apparently, he was the first to join the Cardston Troop in the "C" squadron, 13 regiment C. M. R. (Canadian Mounted Rifles) at Cardston, Alberta, Canada, at C. O. E. F., at Calgary.

The local newspaper ran a story about the war and Cosley being the first to join the war effort. Joe's friends were excited for him and felt Cosley was a hero for deciding to go. He certainly was brave to be going. Cosley didn't have a wife and family, he was an expert rifleman and Indian fighter so he was in a better situation than most.

Joe was known for having good luck and being able to land on his feet in troubled times. This winter proved to be very lucky for Joe. He traded one uniform for another and even received a new hat. He was on the payroll, had a place to stay and meals to eat. Everyone likes a solid man in uniform and people liked Joe in his.

Training

It took a long time for the government to get ready for this war. Weeks turned into months and the Cardston soldiers were still in Canada training. Joe and his comrades trained in Cardston first. He also trained in Calgary, Lethbridge and Medicine Hat.

Canada, like many other countries, was thrown into a war that it was not prepared for. It took Canada a long time to get ready for the flood of fresh volunteers. It took time to uniform, house, train and provision all the troops. Then it took some time to purchase all the horses the army needed for the mounted troops.

Over There

We do not know exactly when Joe and the others from the Cardston district left for England, but we do have some guidelines. An acquaintance of Cosley had dinner with Joe in Medicine Hat and spent the day with the 13th Overseas Mounted Rifles at the barracks on November 15, 1915.[45]

John Orville Bates reports that he turned 18 in December 1915, before the Cardston boys shipped out, and he was able to go with them. He was assigned to the "A" Squadron and Cosley was in the "B" Squadron in the Fort Gary Horse.

---

[45] Ralf McLain's letter to Norton Pearl, "Backcountry Ranger, The Diaries and Photographs of Norton Pearl," 1994.

Bates continues, "I went over (to England) in the summer of 1916 and was hit at Lone Tree in 1917 when I was 19 years old." The injury landed him in the hospital in London, England.

While there, "I got a letter from Joe Cosley, he wrote quite poetically. I wish I had that letter. I read it so many times that I can remember part of it. Referring to this Lone Tree location, Joe Cosley, and Tom Brown, who was with him, said, "We raided that Lone Tree. Tom had a torpedo to blow up the barb wire in front of the trenches that they were to raid. When the torpedo blew, I let out my war cry." And Joe wrote what his war cry was. And Cosley says, "Tom answered it, and I knew that he was not yet tickling the feet of the hosts of the underworld." "We carried out our objective and left many dead and took some prisoners."

Bates remembers that, "Joe Cosley used to like to chew tobacco and when I'd write home for parcels, and my Dad sent me parcels, he'd send me chewing tobacco to give to Joe."

When Bates returned to France in the winter of 1918, the Germans put on a push in the spring. The Allied side rushed our troops in to hold the line until they could reorganize. Bates' Squadron and Joe's were fighting together. Bates states that one night, "Joe came to me and said he wanted me to go with him." Bates told Cosley that he couldn't do that, couldn't leave my own troop. Cosley said, "You must! We're in deep trouble. I promised your father that I would take care of you and I want you to come with me." Of course Bates couldn't do that but Joe's intentions were good. "Cosley was protective of Bates," adds Jack Holterman who also interviewed Bates.

Bates now understood that Joe Cosley wrote him that letter as if the raid had been in vengeance for me getting hit. "And I didn't know the interest he had in me at that particular time. Cosley was thinking of me, you see. So, I had a lot of respect for Joe Cosley. He was quite a character."

Yes, Cosley was character and the most famous rascal in Glacier Park history. And he was the public's favorite.

After A Long Wait

Eventually Cosley and his army buddies were in France seeing more action than they wanted to. The first soldier from the Cardston area killed in World War I was Sergeant Henry "Harry" Carl Briggs. He died on October 8, 1916,[46] in France. He had lived in Woolford, Alberta about 14 miles east of Cardston.

Eventually every family felt the effects of war and personally knew someone who was killed or missing in action. Too many fought too hard and for too long, for us to forget the debt we owe. Ultimately the 1914-1919 Honor Roll included the following from Cardston and area:

Cardston's World War I Honor Role

Lt. Thurber, S	Lt. Dower, A
Lt. Mountainhorse, A	Sgt. Devonish, H
Sgt. Briggs, H	Cpl. Broadhead, C
Pte. Jackman, A	Pte. Jensen, A
Pte. Woodward, W	Pte. Booth, R
Pte. Sorensen, N	Pte. Gales, A
Pte. Roberts, J	Pte. Leavitt, W
Pte. Sibley, W	Pte. Gooding, C
Pte. Comingsinger, G	Pte. Goacher, W

The War Closed

Bates said: "The war ended at 11:00 on November 11, 1918. We were almost in action then or we would have been shortly. We had a motorcyclist come up with a wire or message for our Commanding Officer, and I was right in front of the column. And they stopped the column and gave him the message. And the Armistice had been signed.

"Our aeroplane had been out scouting and came back and landed in the field alongside us. I remember him showing the officers the bullet holes in the plane where he had been shot at. And we were almost in combat. Another two hours and we would probably have been in action again. But that was the morning the Armistice had been signed (November 11, 1918)," stated Bates

Some of the Indians from the Blood Reserve went to France with different outfits than the Cardston boys. Bates said, "One of the Indians was decorated for bravery. They were willing to go and fight. When asked if Joe Cosley was decorated, Bates said, "No."

The war was over at different times for different troops. We don't know exactly when the Cardston soldiers returned. Yet we do know Cosley returned to Cardston a month later than the general group.

"We won the war," said John Bates, "and came home." "We were so glad the war was over. We'd had enough. It's hard . . . coming home

---

[46] Taken from the war memorial in Cardston located on the corner near the old Court House. Currently the building houses a Museum.

and taking a discharge and settling back into civilian life. It's a difficult thing. You are trained for war and that is all you can think about. We weren't home a month before we were looking for war because that's all we knew. We wanted war."

When Joe Cosley returned to Cardston the first place he went was to the Cardston News.[47] Fred Burton said that Joe came in to see him with this big story of life on the battle front. Joe told Fred that he wanted to be paid for this exclusive war story of a local hero and that was that.

Fred said that he explained to Joe that the paper had no money to pay for stories, and after reading over Joe's paper Fred told him there were many things the paper would have to leave out.

The Cardston News did not print Joe's story, and Cosley went to Calgary where the Calgary Albertan did. It appeared on March 8, 1919 with the title of *FORMER COWPUNCHER AND PIONEER TELLS OF ONE DAY AT THE FRONT: Trooper Cosley, of Cardston, After Being Mixed Up in Adventures All His Life, Takes Part in Great Adventure; He Describes a Warm Day in Fighting.*

> Cavalry work and shooting came easy for Trooper Cosley for he was formerly a scout with a regiment of U.S. cavalry under General Wilson A. Miles, who directed his troops against Sitting Bull, who was killed in that maneuver in 1890. Cosley was also for some time a park ranger in the Glacier National Park, and his outdoor and adventurous career stood him in good stead in many of his close calls while serving at the front.
>
> Here is Trooper Cosley's description of one day at the front. He said: "I was awakened with a drowsiness by the unusual racket of strange men scattered about me, as they were getting up at a nightly hour in the morning. R. C. H. A. had been in action since midnight, and were still carrying on in the sunken road, 50 yards from where I laid. . . .
>
> The article was detailed but even with all the action, Cosley still notes what happened when during a lull.
>
> "The weather was still fine at 4:30 p.m. Conditions looked favorable to us; due likely to a lull in battle activity. Warlike appearances now seemed greatly modulated, and the birds were singing in the air and men hummed familiar airs."

---

[47] Fred Burton, Interviews with the author starting in September, 1957 after an article on Joe Cosley ran in the Lethbridge Herald.

CHAPTER 9

THE GROWING GLORY DAYS

The war was over and Cosley returned to prime development in th tourist trade. There were four new Chalets built during the war or shortl afterwards. Joe was to soon discover that his traplines would bring in bigger harvest than before the war. The economy was booming and folk were starting to travel.

Glacier and Waterton Parks were growing and becoming grea tourist places. Tourists equal opportunities to get hired on to guide all those rich green horn dudes. Cosley was known for being a great guide. He had shown Glacier National Park to some very high and important people over his many years with the Park Service.

Let's review some of the improvements that were developing in post-war Glacier.

Saddle Horse Operators

One of the largest saddle horse businesses that operated within Glacier was the Park Saddle Horse Company,[48] based in Babb. They expanded operations from Many Glacier Hotel as the Bar X 6 Ranch, and eventually had 1,000 head of horses in the park. They were the largest such outfit in the world, and 10,000 guests or visitors rode the trails of Glacier on their horses each season for many years.

Their new concept was to build permanent tent camps for the following locations: Fifty Mountain, Goat Haunt, and Cosley Lake.[49]

---

[48] Donald H. Robinson, *Through The Years In Glacier National Park*, 1960

[49] The wood frame platform for the tents was constructed above the trail about a quarter of mile from the lake. It provided a commanding view of not only Cosley Lake; you could see all the way to Pyramid Peak and lots of mountains beyond.

The trip started and ended with Many Glacier Hotel and included Granite Park Chalet; it became known and marketed as the North Circle Trip. Most trips were based on one night in each of the five locations.

The expansion of the automobile and bus systems cut into the back country trips, and by 1942 the Bar X Six was down to 5,000 per year.

Bill Montgomery (tourist) watching Thompson's "Move Camp" from Elizabeth Lake to Cosley Lake. Notice the diamond hitch on the boxes. Picture courtesy of Oaklie Thompson

The Bell Ringers

In tune with the old Swiss tradition of having bells which hikers or riders could ring out in celebration of their mountain climb, the Great Northern Railway people got together with the Glacier Park Hotel Company to request that locomotive bells be mounted at summits on major mountain sites. One such location was Stoney Indian Pass.

These were high quality bells made of thick bronze. In the early 1920's they cost the Great Northern about $200 each at the factory, in addition to crating, shipping and mounting.

It was a thrill to ring the bell and a status symbol to become a "Bell Ringer" in Glacier National Park.

Motor Boat Excursions

The third commercial transportation was by boat. This gave city folk an opportunity to see the park from the water.

The boats were designed and built under the strict standards and approval of the U.S. Coast Guard. Licensed captains skippered each vessel with regular inspections of both captains and vessel. Boat tours increased. Even tourists not staying at a park hotel took the boat to see the sights.

In 1927 and 1928, Captain Billy Swanson, a boat builder and operator on Flathead Lake, built the "International" for the Glacier Park Hotel. The International operated only on Waterton Lake and began service in the summer of 1928. This boat is still in operation today. It's length along the water line is 73 feet and the beam is 16 feet. It is a twin screw, with double engines and was licensed to carry 250 passengers.

Passengers today prefer the scenic top deck, but on colder days you'll find most below.

"On the Trail" Canadian Work Camp in 1924.
Harden West, Charlie Findlay, Oaklie Thompson.
Picture courtesy of Oaklie Thompson

Combination Trips

With the addition of the "International" tourists were able to take a spur trip via the International and stay at the Prince of Wales Hotel overlooking Waterton. A shuttle bus returned them back to Many Glacier Hotel. A round trip deal.

Shorter trail trips could then be scheduled from Many Glacier Hotel via Ptarmigan Tunnel and Elizabeth Lake to the Cosley Tent Camp. After a two or three night stay, they continued over Stoney Indian Pass, rang the bell, then at Goat Haunt boarded the International for the highlight trip of the day. That night they could dine European style and sleep at the Prince of Wales Hotel. Many would then stay a few days to see more of Waterton Lakes before returning state side.

Canadian Whisky Comforts at Cosley Lake

During the hay days of the Great Northern Railway in Glacier, enterprising Canadians[50] willing to take advantage of a desire for liquor, started supplying Belly River.

Two such horsemen sometimes took one bottle of whisky first to the ranger station to see if Hockett was there. If they found him they offered him a drink or two or more. The two Canadians would then want to leave to go home. Of course, they really planned to go to the Bar X Six camp at Cosley Lake and sell the whisky to all the wealthy big city guests there.

But when they wanted to take the bottle with them, Hockett would stop them and say, "You are not allowed to have that bottle in the Park. You'll have to leave it here at the station." And Hockett kept the bottle and kept drinking. That is just what the horsemen wanted.

The two entrepreneurs would then ride their liquor-laden horses to Cosley Lake, unpack their saddle and duffel bags, sell all the bottles they had brought with them and take orders for their next trip.

By 1927 they had a regular thing going with the kitchen people at the Bar X Six camp at Cosley Lake. It was a major summer activity, a cash crop for all connected to the distributions of Canadian whisky.

Even Lake McDonald was supplied via Ahern Pass. Their secret success was to pack each bottle so it would never directly touch another, preventing the clinking glass sound that could break the bottle or alert the authorities.

They never got caught, and they earned lots of money to better their ranches back in Alberta.

Cosley Cave and Sulfur Springs

"I've never seen Cosley Cave," states Jack Holterman, "but I've been told it does exist. It contains Indian picture-writing on the inside walls and therefore is not publicized for fear of vandalism." Jack adds, "Other caves in Glacier Park are usually reserved for scientific study rather than for tourism. There are also sulfur springs in the area of Cosley Cave."

Apparently, these sulfur springs are not hot springs or more people would have discovered them. It could also be that the petroglyphs carved

---

[50] Private conversations with different residents of Southern Alberta.

or painted on the inner cave walls were considered sacred or holy by the Indians.

Joe Cosley saw the opportunity of a lifetime. Here were rich folks traveling to places they have never been before, and Joe could speak their language. The first thing Joe did was to sell the tourist potential of his Cosley Cave. He wrote to the head of the Park Saddle Horse Company offering his unique talents and the opportunity to add the Cosley Cave to the horse trips. Cosley wrote four or so letters, but the saddle horse outfit did not hire Cosley. It looked like either Cosley had asked for too much money or the horse outfit realized there was no Cosley Cave.

Joe's New Cash Crop

But that did not stop Joe. He just showed up at Cosley Lake in July and August each summer and engaged the wealthier tourists to see the park, "Cosley Style" for his extra charge. He had takers and he was busy with people waiting for his next tour. The trail crew said Cosley had tourists lined up waiting for Joe to return and take them.[51]

Joe Cosley met some very important people touring in the back country and obviously they were impressed with him as an expert guide. Guiding tourists was only a summer job and a rewarding pastime between trapping seasons for Cosley.

Lloyd Sanders of Cardston remembers he first helped his father Thomas Julius "Duke" Sanders freight in supplies to the Cosley Camp during the early summer. The river was high and floated the wagon with the current. He says tourists came to Cosley Camp by horse over the pass to stay at the camp for a few days at a time. Lloyd doesn't remember which pass, but thinks it was Stoney Indian Pass. With friends helping friends, assisting the tourists was benefiting everyone.

Always A Trapper

Towards the end of the 1920's Cosley had started prospecting and perhaps trapping further north than ever before with success, but he still returned to Belly River in Glacier and Waterton Parks.

When Joe was at Nordegg, Alberta (119 miles west of Red Deer on Hwy. 11) he wrote a letter to Mrs. Margaret Ivins in Cardston, stating he was "anxious to start for the camps," to get started trapping. Joe asked her to write letters to him there since he was going to be setting out in a day or two, and that he would turn his horses loose at the cabin so they would find the place they winter.

---

[51] In conversation with Oaklie Thompson and Eddie Ivins.

Perhaps Joe didn't stay in Nordegg for the trapping season as suggested in an unpublished letter entitled, Canadian Trapper Pretender. Several things may not be right with this message to his long-time friend Margaret. If the "pretender" letter is true, Joe quietly returned to Cardston and found a partner to grubstake the winter's trapping. It looks like Cosley did not want his Margaret to find out he was in Cardston and Mountain View area and not in Nordegg. It was like Cosley to do this when he had reasons to.

He also may not have had any horses. His last two horses died after falling from Ahern Pass when they slipped on the ice and loose rock that broke away under foot.

> Ranger Cosley, under date of July 6, when returning to his station after a conference at headquarters, attempted Ahern Pass. While crossing the pass, a snow-covered ledge broke off and he narrowly escaped with his life. The horse he was riding and his pack horse were instantly killed, falling hundreds of feet into the canyon beneath. [52]

Cosley retrieved what he could, which included his fancy saddle.

This horse could have been Joe's last horse as he sold this saddle and other tack he salvaged shortly afterwards.

Did Cosley Have Trapping Pardners?

Many people have said that Joe Cosley always trapped alone and never had a partner. They state he liked the seclusion of being alone.

Frank Goble,[53] now of Cardston, states that, "Charlie Nixon was Joe Cosley's partner on a trapline on the Sage Creek, just north of Waterton Park. They operated together in that locations for two years."

Frank is no stranger to trapping. He has written three books about his own trapping entitled, "The Trapper."[54] I recommend the books and the writer. He has seen and admired some of Joe's marten sets in the Waterton and Glacier areas and he marvels at those classic sets.

Frank was 5 or 6 when he met Cosley. Cosley liked to play baseball in Aetna. Joe played Right Field and Frank's dad was First Base.

"About 1920," Frank reminded me, "Joe Cosley was headquartered in the Akamina Valley about 2 miles below Akamina Pass. He did some

---

[52] R. H. Chapman, Report of the Acting Superintendent of the Glacier National Park to the Secretary of the Interior, 1912 (Washington Government Printing Office. 1912, p 10.)

[53] In a conversation with the author in April, 1998.

[54] See information on "The Trapper" page 181.

of his trapping around Cameron Lake in Waterton Lakes National Park. Bo Holroyd, later the Chief Warden, and Wallace Gladstone, spent a hard day on Joe's trail in the Cameron Lake, Boundary Creek area, trying to catch him, which they never did. Following his trail through the pass and down to his cabin, the two weary Wardens were met at the door of the cabin by Joe who laughingly said: 'How come you boys took so long to get here" I've had supper cooked for two hours!' The two Canadian Wardens spent the night there with Joe. When they left the next morning, Bo told Joe: 'One of these times we'll catch you!' They never did, but Joe Heimes managed to do so."

Joe Cosley, in the center, and Morris Moscovich, in the black suit with cane. Morris, a business man from Lethbridge, would seasonally drive his black car to J. J. West's to buy fur from Joe Cosley. It was a direct purchase. Joe received more for his harvest, and Morris paid less than he would have buying from the buyers. The man wearing the vest was the driver.
Picture Courtesy of Richard West

Cosley was known to have sold his prime furs at different places ranging from Pincher Creek, Fort Macleod, Lethbridge, Cardston and Medicine Hat, all in Alberta to Winnipeg, Manitoba and points even further east.

The fact of the matter is that Joe did sell in different places. He seemed easy-going and let money slip through his fingers, as the saying goes. However, to Cosley, furs were all business. He soon discovered that he could cut out the middle man and go directly to a buyer and get a much better price for his hard work. Morris Moscovich was one such buyer who paid Joe much higher prices for his season's take.

Summertime

With the annual trapping season over and his pockets full of cash, Joe found the chance to get away, visit friends and prospect areas new and old. Some time each summer, he would make the trek over the mountain to Columbia Falls and visit with friends in this booming town.

While in Columbia Falls, he would stay at the Gaylord Hotel ear the Great Northern Railway. While staying at the hotel, Cosley 'ould spot a tourist and engage him with one of the Cosley stories. Often ıe guest would want to hear more and take Joe to lunch to hear the conclusion of a story started and perhaps hear another experience.

"The hotel was a meeting place for people. Not only was the lobby full of visitors but so was the front porch," said Dorothy Brading,[55] who knew Cosley since she was a teenager.

The Rexall Drug Store was across the street from the hotel and Joe often went over and talked to young Dorothy who worked there. She still remembers him leaning on the high counters and telling one adventurous story after another. She will never forget the "beautifully done pictures" Cosley drew in his journals and that he had several such journals. He used crayons to draw soft pastel colors that brought out the colors of the mountains and the wildlife. He also used finer charcoal leads. Joe had some of his stories typed up by Dorothy's sister in Columbia Falls.

Photo of Joe's ranger cabin in Belly River, found in *History of Mountain View*
Courtesy of Cardston & District Historical Society

---

[55] Dorothy Brading lived in Columbia Falls, Montana. She was 90 years old and had a sharp memory when I interviewed her in 1997.

CHAPTER 10

BELLY RIVER RANGER STATION:

BR Station, Winter. Picture courtesy of Joe Heimes, circa 1927

Introduction

Joe Heimes was the Park Ranger in Belly River for 23 years. He started when snowshoes were the standard mode of transportation (the use of skis was controversial and their practicality a matter of debate).

His story has an authenticity that could not have been duplicated by anyone else. Even though some of the details of his life may seem to some mundane, his work in the Rockies was exciting and shocking.

Heimes has shared gems from both the extraordinary events and the routine.

Joe Heimes is the first to admit that his only claim to fame was his connection to the events surrounding the capture and trial of the first Belly River ranger, the famous Joe Cosley. Heimes recognized that the other Joe's work began when — and he notes the irony — rangers were urged to hunt predators[56] and were required to kill elk and deer for their own food supply. At the same time they were to conduct vigorous patrols to find and charge other hunters who crossed into the park, sometimes unknowingly. Heimes also recognized that when the park policy changed, Cosley should have complied.

Heimes was the longest serving ranger stationed at Belly River. He was assigned to other districts for a few years, then re-assigned to Belly River. The "jewels" were exciting there also. For example, at one point Heimes drove past a tourist feeding a bear from the window of his car. Heimes stopped, walked back and told the tourist he had to stop feeding the bear because it was against the park rules. The warning was not accepted. When Heimes threatened to arrest the tourist his message was accepted and the tourist drove away — leaving Heimes "nose to nose with a bear expecting to be given another sandwich."

Heimes' story is a history lesson offered by a participant. It has a flavor and flair that is, well, ranger-like.

Joe Heimes History [57]

Heimes was born in Racine, Wisconsin, the same day President McKinley was assassinated, September 6, 1901. His parents were Mathias and Katherine Heimes.

Joe worked in Palo Alto, California, at the government Veterans Hospital from 1919 to 1923 as the Commissary Clerk. His duty was to dispense groceries and supplies needed to feed over 2,000 hospital patients and several hundred medical staff. The facility was established in rows and rows of old army barracks that held about 40 soldiers in each barracks. He said, "It was a real good job. It was like being at home because we ate, slept and played there. There were no problems at all."

---

[56] Chauncy "Chance" Beebe, one of the early Glacier Park Rangers, often referred to as "Old Man Beebe," in which Beebe Flats was named after him. He later worked for the Department of the Interior as a Predator Control Officer and was said to have shot and killed more than 300 bears, both black and grizzly. It was he who killed the famous "Medicine Grizzly" of Blackfoot lore. There are Beebes living on the Blood Reserve north of Cardston.

[57] Sections regarding Joe Heimes were recorded by the author between 1989 and 1993.

During off hours Joe worked out at the athletic club boxing; he could box fairly well. In 1923 the talk of the country was the upcoming Dempsey / Givens fight in Shelby, Montana.

Heimes decided to quit the hospital and head for Shelby.

Let's drop in and listen to Joe Heimes reveal how it all happened:

I packed my packsack and headed for the railway yards and started on the freight trains going to Montana. I arrived in Shelby over a week before the fight and watched Jack Dempsey every day at his training camp just out of town. I never sparred with Dempsey, but decades later I did spar with Ingermar Johansson who was the world boxing champion. Ingemar, Alan Ladd, Sidney Poitier and James Darren were in Glacier Park with a movie outfit filming, *All The Young Men,* while I was stationed at St. Mary. I'm getting ahead of myself.

The day after the Dempsey fight I grabbed a freight train and went to Glacier Park. I worked for the park until 1962. I worked there so long that I figured that I owned part of it. When I retired I was the oldest one and now I am 30 years older[58].

When I first got to Park headquarters George Snider was there. The front end was the bunk house, the middle was the park office, and the other end was the cook house.

My first assignment at Glacier National Park was at Polebridge. I built a fire lookout at Polebridge and worked on trails that summer. I also helped build a telephone line down to the Camas Creek Entrance Station.

I loved the outdoors and adored Glacier Park. The only drawback was, being new with no seniority, only being employed during the summer and fall.

In 1924 I was sent to Huckleberry to build another lookout, other buildings, and, as always, trail assignments.

After I built Huckleberry Mountain lookout, Jack Wooder and I built Indian Ridge lookout and other buildings.

In those years I was on the fire lookout and was a temporary ranger, not permanent. I wasn't permanent until I went to Kishenehn in the spring of 1925.

What is a park employee to do all winter long when not working for the park? I didn't like being laid off for the winter and early spring. One

---

[58] Recorded August, 1993 at Joe Heimes cabin on Flat Head Lake. His address: P. O. Box 27, Somers, MT 59932, and his neighbor (and landlord's) phone number was 1 (406) 757-3329.

winter I returned to California and worked at the Veterans Hospital. The next I stayed in Kalispell working at odd jobs.

My break came early in 1925. I was called to go to Kishenehn to replace MacAfee. The guy up at Kishenehn, MacAfee, committed suicide about February or so. MacAfee was not the type to be put up in a place like that. Loneliness and other reasons.[59]

"I was assigned a permanent Ranger Station at Nyack later that summer, where I built several buildings and was ready for winter," ends Heimes.

Ranger at Belly River

It is quite a story of why (or how) Heimes first went into Belly River. Belly River was a permanent station, year-round operation summer and winter. The story starts with the previous Belly River Ranger, from 1921 through 1925, H. C. Hockett, who liked to drink. Hockett didn't like the long, long winters in the isolation of Belly River. He didn't like the company of himself even in the summers, but at least there were visitors in the summer. There is a popular story in Alberta of one time that Cosley met Hockett on the trail in Belly River. Cosley told him, "If I ever catch you on the Belly River trails again, I will kill you." As much as this sentence sounds familiar, Hockett was in the drinking establishments in Canada even more.

Back in those days there was no direct communications from Belly River to park headquarters, just the Canadian postal service, and that was slow. So all winter long the park didn't know if Hockett was alive or dead in Belly River, except at the end of every month when a report was to be sent in. Heimes recalls, "we got all our mail once a month for decades at Mountain View, Alberta on the Canadian side."

Heimes continues his story.

Even though Hockett was in Lethbridge drinking, he had a deal with the storekeeper and post master in Mountain View to send in Hockett's monthly Belly River report. Hockett would either do the reports up several months in advance and leave them with the storekeeper, or he would mail his reports in to the Post Master, at Mountain View who would remail each report on time to GNP headquarters with the stamp post-marked from Mountain View.

---

[59] See also Montana's Early-Day Rangers by Robert C. (Bert) Gildart, published by Montana Magazines, Inc. 1985, page 81 for additional information about MacAfee's suicide at Kishenehn.

For years headquarters would get the report and thought all was well. Headquarters was supposed to get the report between the 3rd and the 5th of the following month. If the roads to Lethbridge were bad in the winter, then Hockett would get to Calgary or Waterton or any place where there was liquor.

This apparently went on for months at a time for years. Hockett stayed away from Belly River for long periods, and only returned to Mountain View from his drinking binges to pick up his mail and his pay-checks mailed from Park Headquarters.

Many times when Hockett was drinking he would get nasty and mean and would start fighting. The reports of his arrest made it back to Glacier. Maybe the Mounted Police in Waterton or the city police in Lethbridge phoned the Park to notify that Hockett was locked up for fighting and drunkenness. Or perhaps the Canadian law enforcers filed their reports with Ottawa and the Canadian government contacted Washington who passed the message to Glacier to get Hockett out of Belly River so he couldn't go into Canada and drink.

I was in Nyack Creek (west of the divide, contributory to the middle fork Flathead River) at the time. I was one of the few single rangers in the park. Of course, for something like this situation, the park picks on the single rangers. They were afraid of ranger's wives, you know. Wives would not put up with the winters in a remote places like Belly River.

I went into Belly River on the 5th of December 1925. I had previously just moved from Kishenehn station to Nyack about two months before. I was all set nice for the winter there. I had chopped and stacked all my firewood. I had lots of my food in for the winter. I had built a new root cellar and put a new roof on the Nyack station. We had to do that work ourselves in those days. They don't have to do it nowadays. Today, everything is done by outside contract: materials, carpenters, painters and bringing in supplies — everything.

We used to build all our own buildings in the park. We cut our own timber. We had a sawmill at Fish Creek. I worked at that sawmill for three months one fall. We cut our own lumber for the building we built in the park. Not any more.

In 1925 the Chief Ranger had asked two or three other fellows before they asked me. They hesitated about sending me into Belly River because I was one of the newer rangers. On top of that, I was what they would call, a kid, see. I was young. I was new at the game. Two years experience on the fire lookouts and on trails and on the roads and then time at the sawmill at Fish Creek and work at Nyack. I only had three years experience in the park before Belly River.

I don't know how they ever figured that I was the type to go to Belly River in the wintertime. Nobody moves into Belly River — not in the middle of the winter.

It was an emergency. They had to get Hockett out of jail in Canada and they had to find some other place in the park to put Hockett. They were desperate to find somebody to man Belly River immediately.

The park had to find someone who was willing to go to Belly River. They asked Fordy Lawrence, he was a bachelor. He was at Logging Creek. They also asked two other fellows. No one would ever volunteer to go into Belly River, not even the single rangers. Lawrence was more of the type of guy to go into a place like Belly River. He had been working in the park for six years, three of them as Ranger at Logging Creek. Nobody would go.

So I was the last resort. I was at Nyack. I had mixed feelings about Belly River. I wanted to go, but not until spring. I wanted to go because Nyack was right on the railroad and I didn't like those trains going through all day and night. The station was right on the river (Middle Fork Flathead) then so you could look up the track and see the trains coming for quite a ways. I didn't like the train whistle. My whole idea to work at Glacier in the first place was getting away from automobiles, trains and people and everything else.

1929 Model A Chevrolet at Belly River Ranger Station
Picture courtesy of Owen McClung

So I told Chief Carter that I wanted to go to Belly River but not till spring. I was all settled there at Nyack. I went to a lot of work to get ready for the winter.

"Well," he said, "Whoever goes to Belly River will stay there if he wants to stay there." I told him under those conditions I would go because I wanted Belly River. I had heard what a nice place it was. It was as far away from the headquarters as you could get and still stay in the park, see. Belly River was away from all the top brass from Park Headquarters bothering you and yet it was so very beautiful. Just like old Hockett with his monthly reports, nobody knew where he was. He could have been in Paris and still got his report sent in from Mountain View. Hockett had a good thing going. Of course, Belly River had no trains, day or night, to rumble and scream past you.

So I got packed and ready to go to Belly River. That was a job to go into Belly River. I left Nyack near the end of November.

It was cold then and that was on the west side. I was soon to find out how cold it can get on the east side.

I sent all my stuff on the railroad. At the time there was no highway to the Belly River District. I went with my gear to East Glacier by train. The park had a truck driver at East Glacier that was off duty but they hired him specially to pick up my stuff and take me as far as he could get to the end of the road — trailhead to Belly River. At that time as far as you could drive to was to John J. West's between Mountain View and Waterton Park on the Canadian side of the border.

I was new to the country. We had a flat tire near Duck Lake and that took time. At the Canadian Boundary we had to leave my gear at the border and go into Cardston with the assistant chief ranger in his Model T to get the Mounted Police and bring him back to border station because the Mountie had to escort the gear and me all the way through that part of Alberta, Canada, and up to the U. S. Border going into Belly River. My stuff was held "in bond" they said.

We got to John J. West's, and I didn't even know where Belly River was. Of course, John J. was a big help. For some reason either he didn't want to go up with me or wasn't available at the time. He had other things to do. But he said he would get a good man. He said Duke Sanders lived out of Mountain View a little way, and he would probably take us in.

And so we got in touch with Duke Sanders and he said sure, he would take my stuff in. Duke said it would be a tough trip into Belly River that time of year, and there was a blizzard coming on. But we had to go. Duke brought his son Lloyd to help him with the team and wagon.

The rivers were already starting to ice up. We had two fords of the Belly River to go over on the Canadian side and two more on our side. The ice was thick on the river banks but open in the middle so it was tricky crossing the river by horse and pack horse four times during that storm.

And so the Mounted Police went as far as the boundary line, then. of course, he could go back. I even had to hire a saddle horse from West's so the Mountie could escort my stuff right to the U. S. Border. Duke and I went the rest of the way. The truck driver stayed at West's.

The Mountie returned to West's, turned the saddle horse in and returned to Cardston with the Park truck driver. Duke, Lloyd and I continued and went on up to the station. We got there in the dark. This was in the old station. We got my things unpacked from the wagon and I started to check things out. It was cold. I was in real trouble. There wasn't enough wood cut to even start a fire in the stove! I was mad.

The logs were all there because Al Thompson, who did all the trail work in Belly River for Hockett, had cut and hauled logs to the station. Hockett was to have cut the logs and split them into firewood. It was obvious that Hockett had not been in the station for months. I had to saw some logs then split them to get enough firewood to at the fire in the stove going. Duke finished with the horses while I got supper on.

Duke Sanders had previously figured on staying over night but the way the blizzard was going he said he would just rest his horses an hour or two and head on back. There were lots of oats up there, thanks to Al Thompson. Duke said he was going to get out of there tonight because if they didn't get out tonight they probably would be here with me all winter long. So we got something to eat and got warm and then they saddled up and harnessed up the horses and got the hell out of there.

So there I was. The 5th of December in a blizzard that lasted weeks and I was without any winter wood cut and stacked. It was a strange country. The only reason I knew it was Belly River is because Duke had brought me there. I was sure lost. I was 24 years old at the time. And to be put in a place like that at that time of year?

It first snowed for three days and four nights and tapered off. Then the high winds started to really blow. Then another storm hit and repeated the welcome just for me.

What had I agreed to? I quickly learned that the eastern slope of the continental divide was *much colder* that the west side.

It took me six days to shovel my path to the outhouse. It had not been cleared that winter.

"That is how I went into Belly River against my will," said Heimes with a tiny smile on his face.

CHAPTER 11

MY FIRST WINTER IN BELLY RIVER

Belly River Ranger Station, winter 1925-1926
Picture courtesy of Joe Heimes

As a writer, I was fascinated to learn what life was like at the station and around Belly River in the winter time. Hope you will get the same charge out of Heimes telling us his unique story in the backcounty of Glacier National Park.

Heimes continues his exciting story.[60]

[60] Interviews recorded with Joe Heimes between 1989 and 1993

I spent my first night sawing and splitting wood for the stove. I had to get a little bit ahead of the situation. After I had four days worth of wood, cut and stacked, I finally let myself go to sleep. I was up twice feeding that old stove. I needed the heat and I didn't ever want to let the fire go out because the fire wood was not fully dry. This was a long night.

I spent every daylight hour sawing those logs, splitting and hauling firewood and cleaning up after Old Man Hockett. Then I stacked all the cut wood in the cabin or in the barn. The horses also needed attention.

The nights were long, dark, and loud with all natural sounds in the winter. There would be an occasional coyote or wolf howl in the evening from the ridge to the west or south, but it was the unrelenting wind that pounded the door and rattled the frost-covered windows that bothered me the most. But I kept warm.

Outhouse
Picture courtesy of Joe Heimes

My nightly routine would be to keep the fire blazing away while I made supper. I sometimes even baked bread in the oven while making stew on top. After supper I would check on the stock, refuel the stove and fill out reports including costs to get me to the ranger station. The Park would be sending a payment check to Duke Sanders. The Park had an arrangement with the general store in Mountain View, Alberta, so I could get supplies (mostly food) and send my mail to the Park.

"I was now a full time Glacier National Park Ranger, permanently stationed at Belly River," proudly remembered Heimes.

Joe Heimes' First Patrol

I had so much catching up to do I could not patrol my district right away. There were vital things I had to do first like get my supply of firewood in shape. For those early days I had a visibility problem — I could hardly see for all the blowing drifting snow.

Finally the day arrived that I could go on patrol. It began at 2:00 a.m. when the wind stopped. The silence was beautiful and I really slept.

I awoke with sun pouring in the window. I had slept in. What a view. I could see for miles. Blue sky, snow capped mountains all around. Stillness covered the valley.

I felt lucky to be the ranger at Belly River.

I did my chores and was off on my first snowshoe patrol of Belly River. I didn't want to go far — just to orient myself. I took a map and went about a mile south then followed the river to the west of the station. What a sight. It was so peaceful.

Then some Ruffed Grouse[61] darted from the snow just in front of me. Damn near scared me to death. I had thought I was the only creature up here except the horses.

There were some other small wildlife signs but mostly me and the new snow fall.

"Before returning to the station I trekked all the way down river to where I thought our last ford was and scouted out the area. I couldn't see any signs of steam rising from the river so I knew it was frozen solid. I could see down the river and into Canada — my next trip if the weather held. I would be ready if it did," said Heimes.

His First Trip To Town

"Maybe the last storm for the winter was over. I was preparing for this trip last night doing my reports up. I was ready. My gear was ready and all the stuff I needed to mail to H.Q. was ready," Heimes remarked.

---

[61] In cold weather, they fly into the soft snow, squirm ahead underneath and make a small cavity and spend the night or nights there in warmth, states Goble.

I was up early and on the trail, so to speak, before the sun lit up the bright snow on Bear Mountain and Sentinel Mountain beyond. These two giants kept me referenced as did Old Chief.

Of course there was no trail with all the snow. I mostly snow-shoed down the river and cut through where I felt I could save time.

I knew I had picked a great day for weather. No wind or clouds and the temperature warmed to -5° F, perfect for hiking on snowshoes. I made it a point to stop every half hour and get my breath and look around and monitor the weather. It was still great.

My most memorable stop was the slash called the line. What a sight today. I could see both directions. Two and a half weeks ago I was at this very spot for my first time, on my way in with Duke. What a busy fortnight it has been.

I was on course and making good time but I had no time to waste. Turns out I was so right.

Just as I approached J. J. West's I saw them leaving. They saw me across the field to the south of them waving and they waited for me.

It was so great to see people again. Not only that, they were good to give me a ride to town with them. They were going shopping and seeing friends in Mountain View. What a break. A double break for me because they knew the way.

We talked. I learned that Duke and Lloyd Sanders made it home safe but the snow was piling up.

Station looking at Bear Mountain in the rear.
Picture courtesy of Joe Heimes

"John told me he didn't want to take me into Belly River because he thought I was too young and he didn't think I would make it through a day up there. I couldn't tell if he was funning me or not. I was just pleased with myself to have made it out on my own in a strange land and to have met them. And I was thrilled to see them and get a ride to town."

Mountain View [62]

Mountain View was named because it has a great view of the Rocky Mountains in Canada. It is a hamlet on the highway between Cardston and Waterton Lakes. Joe Heimes would regularly journey out to Mountain View.

Return with me to his first trip to Mountain View.

The West's took a shortcut further south of the current highway which resulted in less hills and snowdrifts. Over the years in Belly River I always loved to go to Mountain View and I would take this short cut.

When we arrived at Park Strate's (pronounced Strattee) General Store, there were people inside warming their hands around the wood stove. J.J. introduced me and everyone welcomed me to Canada.

I had to do my business so I could return. John West told me I was welcome to stay longer in town and ride back to the ranch with them but he also understood my need to get back to the station before dark.

After getting my reports sent off to Belton I found I even had some mail. I ended up buying more food than I had planned. I saw a sled, or what we call today a toboggan, for sale in the store. Second, someone offered me a Jap orange. It had no seeds and was easy to peel and tasted great. I ended up buying a case of oranges and the toboggan along with my list of things. I was off before noon.

I had had a good first trip. I followed the same shortcut trail the West's did. The broken snow was easy to travel even pulling my new load.

From the West's I followed my tracks back. On my way to Canada I wasn't running so my return was on packed snow. The muscles I used to break snow could rest while I put others to work pulling my load.

It was actually easy to pull this load even with the old blanket I borrowed to tarp down my load to prevent my food from freezing.

When I stopped at the line I wished I had brought my camera. I wish I had a picture of the line that day. It was my first round trip out of

---

[62] Mountain View, (hamlet) 49° 08'N, 113° 36'W. The name is descriptive in that there is great view of the mountains from this locality. Located between Cardston and Waterton.

the park and into Canada. And I wish that someone had taken my picture pulling that sleigh right at that spot.

"After I finished my chores at the station I paused to enjoy a special sunset. A great day for me — a lot of first's," stated Heimes.

It Was Winter Still For Me

"I had not seen my last snow storm," reflected Heimes. When I first got to Belly River I lived in the old Belly River Station. In those early days the snow would drift up behind the Ranger Station clear past the roof. The outhouse was across the creek and I had to shovel snow every morning. The kitchen door was the only door I could get open when it drifted. I got so fed up with trying to get out to the outhouse. Sometimes you have to get out there in a hurry, so I let it drift in. I put a tunnel through the drift.

Nellie resting on the US / Canada Border.
Picture courtesy of Joe Heimes

Over a few days the heat from the kitchen would ice up the tunnel and it made a nice entrance there.

Many people might think that I would just eat and sleep all winter long. Not the case. I probably did more patrolling of that area than any man who was ever in there in the winter time. I used snowshoes. I made a monthly trip to Slide Lake and weekly to Cosley and Glenns Lakes, and to Elizabeth Lake. Sometimes as far as Helen Lake. And then there was my trips out to Mountain View. I patrolled the Belly River District every week of every year I was assigned there.

I quickly learned to pick the weather[63] to travel in. It was all right to travel east up over Gable Mountain to Slide Lake with the wind at my back but coming the other way was hard if there was a west wind blowing. At times, if I was heading west in a hard wind, I would have to crawl on my hands and knees for two miles to get through the open country on top. I learned from that trip and that weather.

My regular route took me east over Gable Pass then I would stay at the cabin down by Slide Lake. The next day I would go around the east side of Chief Mountain and back to Belly River Station. It was a two day trip and I patrolled the area at least once a month year around.

Joe Heimes had many visitors who came to the park just to see him.
He couldn't remember the kid's name but next was
Mrs. Chipps and Marjorie Cheney[64]
Picture courtesy of Joe Heimes

After I learned the ropes I sometimes went the whole way, about 35 miles, in one day. But most Gable trips were two day treks. One time I ran into Mrs. Chipps' cabin at Boundary Creek[65] . I found a good looking

[63] As soon as Joe Heimes could, he arranged to get an AM radio installed at the Belly River Station so he could monitor weather forecasts. He kept the radio tuned to CJOC, 1220 on the dial, a Lethbridge, Alberta station. In the summer evenings when Heimes returned to the cabin he would also listen to the sports casts. He was a big fan of the Milwaukee Brewers baseball team.

[64] See Appendices # 2, page 133

[65] Boundary Creek, 49° 00.00'N, 113° 22'00"W, is much smaller than a hamlet.

gal there by the name of Marjorie Cheney. She was boarding there. She was a school teacher at Boundary Creek.

Mrs. Chipp's ranch was a mile west of Duke Sanders place, but I never stopped in to see him.

Mrs. K. Chipps used to come up in the summer to Belly River once in a while too. Mrs. Chipps liked it up there. I also dated a Findlay[66] girl in Mountain View. I should have married her.

From then on, every time I went on my monthly trip to Slide and around Chief Mountain, I made it a point to stop and check in on her. I was thinking of marrying that girl. I was thinking about marrying quite a few gals but just when I got ready I was transferred to some other part of the park. I lost out on a pretty good girl there.

For all the beauty Belly River offers I still found the winters long, but never lonely. I had my dog Nellie to visit with. I got Nellie from the Canadian liquor runners that used to run the liquor across on our side at Pack Spring. When I was at Kishenehn they gave this dog to me for looking the other way when they went through. I didn't believe in prohibition. I think that was a lousy thing to have prohibition. They should have made drunkenness a crime instead of prohibition.

Dog Team on Patrol
Picture courtesy of Joe Heimes

I kept check on the game, took snow measurements and weather recordings. My patrols were the first Belly River had seen. Joe Cosley

[66] See Appendices # 2, page 134

didn't patrol the district except for his own "scouting out" beaver and other fur bearing animals. Old Man Hockett did not patrol Belly River. He was on one great big drunk. I was the first and I did it regularly.

In the wintertime, when the weather was bad I would only go to Elizabeth once in two weeks. Because the weather could sometimes change into fierce storms, after the first winter I made the Park build us a cabin on the Lee Creek.

This patrol was too big and I complained that it was too far to make in one or sometimes two days when the weather could change all of a sudden. I told Headquarters that I wouldn't make that trip any more unless they built a cabin on Lee Creek. We constructed that cabin the summer of 1927 and it saved my life several times after that.

Cabin Fever?

I never got cabin fever. There was always too much to do. When I wasn't building or repairing I was getting fire wood. When I was snowed-in, I got caught up on my reports and made plans for the future wilderness development of Belly River.

When old Hockett was moved from Belly River to Nyack, he left three of his own horses at the Belly River station. During the winter, Hockett wrote to me and gave me Old Irish if I wanted him. I wanted him. Irish was real good. I had him for three years more in Belly River. Old Irish was 27 years old but was a very reliable horse.

"I had lots of company with my dogs and horses," shared Heimes.

Patrols on Snowshoes by Heimes

Before and after I had the dog team and sleigh, I would take my patrols on snowshoes in the winter. I had two pairs of snowshoes. One was more for cross-country treks than deep loose snow in the brush. I had lots of practice snowshoeing but I never was as good as Cosley. Cosley, I had heard, could run for hours on snowshoes.

My snowshoes were Alaskan Trapper. They were long and narrow with a 6" rise at the tip and maximum flotation area — a design that makes it an excellent shoe for open country and deep powder. Despite its length, this shoe is easy to walk on and will support a heavy load. It allows you to run with very little effort. They were ideal for going up steep slopes and even ski down snowdrifts without tripping and falling.

Winter patrols during December and January were treats because I enjoyed the two Jap oranges I took with me. I would stop and take a break about every hour or so and eat one of these citrus treats. To this day, I still prefer those oranges. They were easy to peel, no seeds, and the taste bursts all over my mouth. They also gave me the needed boost of energy and improved my health.

My Dog Team Trips by Heimes

I bought my dog team, harnesses and sled from the Riviere boys at Pincher Creek, Alberta for $100 for the whole thing. Those dogs were half wolf. Four dogs and the sleigh for $100.00 was a good deal.

The Riviere boys delivered my dog team and sleigh right to my front door in November 1926. They had a second dog team and sleigh and these fellows came in with two teams and outfits, dropped mine off, turned around and went back the same day. It was the only dog team in Glacier Park. Now, the park won't even let a ranger have a dog for a pet.

Over the years, Nellie had about eight pups a year and I usually had eight adult dogs harnessed up.

I took the team of dogs and the sleigh several times a week on patrol. I never took them over Gable Pass. I would snowshoe Gable all by myself. However, I did take them to Elizabeth Lake and on to Helen, to Cosley and Glenns Lakes. And, of course, out to Mountain View to get my mail, groceries and supplies and send my reports in to HQ. The Mail Run to Mountain View was 20 miles one way and I would usually do the trip in one short day. Some times, I would stay over at John J. West's if I had extra food for the dogs. One usual stop on the way would be at the Canadian Belly River Station, which was manned all winter long in those days too. Their station was a couple of miles from the U.S. border. Some years later the Canadians built another station for the Canadian Belly River a little closer to Waterton.

Dog team leaving station on patrol
Picture courtesy of Joe Heimes

The sleigh was 2 feet wide and 7 feet long and it would really travel with those dogs. I would leave early in the morning for Mountain View and arrive in plenty of time to shop at the little store run by Park Strate. I never went on a trip past a store, that I didn't stop to get some groceries. I would get groceries that wouldn't be held over very long like oranges, eggs, bacon and stuff like that. The supplies that I bought would not freeze because I would pick the weather pretty good when I went to town. And I packed them so well, nothing would break or freeze.

Canadians don't have all the grocery items that we do but they do have things we don't. The Jap Oranges (renamed decades later by the Japanese to Mandarin Oranges), were packed in ½ bushel wooden boxes and two boxes were tied together with rope. These oranges arrived on the shelves at Strate's in late November and continued to well after Christmas. Each orange was individually wrapped in green paper for more protection.

Nick Carter, Chief Ranger and Joe Heimes on Cosley Lake with Cosley Ridge and Gable Mountain behind them. 1928 (no other date listed) Notice the sheep skin caps. Picture courtesy of Joe Heimes.

I always bought one case then another about a week later. They taste better than tangerines, peel easier and have no seeds.

I would pick the days that I would travel with the dog team and sled. I liked 15 to 20 degrees above zero (F). That temperature range is good for snowshoeing and dog team traveling. At those temperatures, the snow holds better and makes the run faster for all. When the going was good for the dogs, I would hop on the sleigh.

My dogs put several thousand miles on the sleigh up until the spring of 1929. I then sold the team and sled and gear back to the same people I bought it from and for the same price I paid for them. So, the dog team and sleigh didn't really cost me, just the food the dogs ate.

Visitors From Above

"From time to time, every ranger district received inspections from Head Quarters. Top brass came to see if what we were doing matched the reports we had previously sent to them. They came to check up on us rangers. Maybe the Chief Ranger also had reports to fill out. These visits were never a one-way thing. While Nick Carter was here I showed him what was needed to improve this district and by the time he left for home he understood both Belly River and me," said Heimes.

Dog Food

"In the summer and early Fall I would try to round up and buy five or six horses. Always someone had an old horse or crippled one they could not use. I could get some for nothing and for the others I had to pay a few dollars. I would bring them up to Belly River in the fall. Usually the grazing was good all Fall and most of the winter up there on the flats," continued Heimes.

The wind blows the snow off those big flats up there. Even after a heavy snowfall the wind usually came up and blew the snow off the grass and into the woods. Often all around the station too.

"When my dogs needed some food I would just go down to the field and bring up one of the old fellows and give him a couple of good shots of oats for a day then harvest the horse the next day. It would take one horse a month to feed my dogs. The main reason I sold my dogs and sled was that I had a hell of a time finding feed for my dogs in the summer time. I sold the dog team and sled in the summer time and took them out on a team and wagon," downhearted Heimes said.

CHAPTER 12

SUMMERTIME AT THE STATION, by Heimes

Well, I finally made it through my first winter.

I couldn't have survived without the preparation that Al Thompson and his son Oakley provided to the Belly River Ranger Station. They, and they alone, brought in my winter's firewood supply. They cut and hauled enough timber (deadfall logs and scrap timbers) to keep me warm for two winters. I was so grateful to them.

Old man Hockett was to have sawed the logs to length, chopped them, and stacked the wood close to the station. But, he didn't. The Thompsons saved my life.

There is more. The Thompsons were the main trail crew for the Belly River Station for many years. Sometimes Harden West would also join the crew. When the Park insisted on hiring only Americans, Belly River lost the best trail crew I have ever known.

Those Canadian boys were hard workers and they went beyond the call of duty. They did things for me. One time my phone system broke down and these good Thompsons took a message to headquarters for me. It saved my bacon.

I wouldn't have asked anyone to go over Ahern even when there is a problem but these guys were old hands at Ahern Pass. I told them all to go and make sure that no one had any problems with the trail or the pass. They dropped off my message to West Glacier and nobody at the office asked them any questions so they turned around and came back to Belly River.

Oaklie Thompson, Charles Findley and Al Thompson
Moving Camp. 1926
Picture courtesy of Oaklie Thompson,

"In the Summer of 1926 I made a foot bridge across the Belly River that was wide enough and strong enough for even a horse to cross. In the Winter I would take my horse and sometimes take a spare horse to trade–off breaking trail. I patrolled Elizabeth, Cosley, Glenns and out to Canada with horses in the winter time," said Heimes.

Dawn Mist Falls Arrest

Heimes said, "I arrested five Canadian girls one time for fishing out of season at Dawn Mist Falls. The season was closed just a day before."

He continues. I should have married one of those girls. Any girl who fishes would make a great wife. It was just after the season was over. I told them they were all under arrest for fishing out of season.

So then one of them wanted to know what I was going to do with them, and what under arrest meant.

Well, I hadn't figured it out yet what I was going to do with five girls, so I had to do some quick thinking. We had a good reputation for quick thinking because if we couldn't think of the right answer we would make something up real quick.

I told them what I was going to do with them is find out who was the best cook, that one would have to stay at the station for one month, and cook for the ranger there.

Well, then they all started to argue as to which one was the best cook, who was going to get to stay at the station, and do the cooking.

“What had I started now! I couldn’t have five girls in that kitchen. That would be chaotic with fights, to see who was going to do what. I finally turned them all loose. I would have had a tough time taking five girls to headquarters. That would have been worse than bringing in Cosley,” ends Heimes.

Remote Life As A Belly River Ranger

When Heimes worked year-round he received 28 working days off each year as a vacation. The 28 days off were based on working 5 days a week, every week, to get the 28 days off. Of course, at Belly River, Heimes never worked just 5 days a week. Only the crew worked a 5 day week, but not the ranger. The ranger worked 7 days a week back then.

Then Joe’s humor speaks up and says, “really some of the crew only worked one day a week. Two days before their weekend arrived they were talking about what they were going to be doing on their days off — when they would go to Waterton, see the girls and everything. When they came back on Monday morning at 8 o’clock they weren’t worth a damn for a couple of days because they were talking about the good times they had. Well, about that time the next weekend would be coming up and you couldn’t get nothing out of them. This is the way it was with the college and high school (punks) kids. It wasn’t that way years ago when we got men to do the work.”

“In the 50’s and 60’s,” says Heimes, “when we had to take these boys from the high schools and colleges it was all together different. Uncle Sam wouldn’t get much more that $5.00 worth of work out of a $100 paid. If you counted the damage to tools, broken handles, and lost tools, you’d be out some more. Some broke the handles on purpose to get out of work. They would bring the broken tools into the Ranger Station in the old station we used as a shop. They would lay them on the bench there for somebody else to fix — which would be me. I didn’t like that system.”

Heimes patrolled the North Fork Belly River for several years on a monthly basis in the summer months. There was just no getting in there in the winter time, he explained. He rarely found anyone up there any way in the summer.

The Most Famous Garden by Heimes

Joe Heimes sometimes traded[67] the vegetables and flowers he raised from his garden behind the ranger station for meals and company with the Glacier Park Saddle Horse Company cook at Cosley Camp.

[67] Stated Brian Kennedy of the Hungry Horse News.

“By the time produce arrived in sub zero temperatures at Mountain View, there wasn’t much left of the shipment. There is nothing finer than fresh vegetables or vegetables cooked fresh,” said Heimes. I raised the best onions, carrots, peas, lettuce and a wide variety of flowers. I had a system for planting my garden in rows so the deer didn’t eat all my crop.

People were sent from different parts of Glacier Park and from many towns in Canada just to see my garden. People never saw a garden like that in the mountains. I kept it especially good and they wanted to know if I had a surveyor to lay these lines out. Each row was straight and the weeds were all pulled out and everything.

“No one else wanted to take care of the garden. It always fell to me. Everytime I was re-assigned to Belly River it took me a couple of years to get the garden clean of weeds so the vegetables would grow healthy.”

Joe Heimes’s Garden
Picture courtesy of Joe Heimes

Bears by Heimes

One spring when I arrived at the weather station I saw 4 grizzly bears in the pasture eating the new spring green grass coming up. An old bear and three yearlings just looked up and watched me come in with the team and wagon and they resumed eating. I had a conscientious objector with me for three years during the war to do the trails.

I went in and started getting supper ready, see.

“Pretty soon I heard something against the office door. It was the mother bear up against that door. There was a little window in the top of the door and I could see through. There was that bear looking into the office through that window. There was a screen door outside too and that was hooked so I was safe. I wanted to take a look at a grizzly up close. She was looking at me and I was looking at her. There wasn't a foot between us. She wasn't afraid of me and I wasn't much afraid of her, as long as I was inside.

So then I thought, I am going to put the fear of God into this gal. I am going to slip back the bolt and yank back the door open. I still had the screen door between us. I hollered and she fell backwards off of the porch, then ran like hell down to the gate. She didn't stop until she got out of the fence. Then she turned around and looked. I bet she thought it was a ghost or something. And the three cubs in the pasture were watching her and she must have said, "come on boys, let's get out of here, this isn't a very good place.

Swimmer At Elizabeth Lake

Another girl I almost arrested was swimming in her birthday suit.

This girl had come from Cosley Camp. She had been staying there for a couple of nights and was waiting for her parents to show up. It was a saddle horse party. She had come ahead of time and with nothing to do over there, so they sent her into Elizabeth Lake for the day.

While she was waiting for her parents she thought, well, it was a warm day, she would go in swimming for a few minutes. I just happened to be on the way up on my patrol and I caught this here girl standing in that cold water up to her waist.

She heard me, turned and saw me, she covered up herself.

Right at the foot of Elizabeth Lake after the stream empties from the lake there are some shallow pools of water with an almost sandy bottom. It is so clear and the shallows makes it look like it is warm.

I told her it was against the law. I didn't make the law because I didn't like the law myself. I was in favor of people swimming whenever they wanted, bathing suits or not. I was in favor of giving people more freedom.

Pretty soon I saw she was getting cold. I could tell it in her speech. She started to shiver. Ten minutes is about as long as someone would want to stay in those waters.

So I started to feel sorry for her. I told her then, Okay, I am going to ride up above for maybe 400 yards to check on the campgrounds at Elizabeth Lake and in the meantime you come out and get dressed but be sure to stay here because you are under arrest. And you can't get away because I am riding a horse.

So she did. I returned in about 30 minutes and she was dressed and sitting on a log by the stream. By the time we got chewing the rag I told the girl that I was not going to arrest her. Then she wanted me to go back to Cosley Lake with her and have supper at the Bar Six Camp.

Two wagon loads of supplies from Belton via J. J. West for the Belly River Ranger Station
Picture courtesy of Richard West

Now you would hardly find one girl hiking by herself. They have got people so damned scared about the bears; some are afraid to go into Belly River backcountry anymore.

I would not be afraid to go through Belly River. I have been in there, I guess, for 25 years and I cannot think of one time that a bear ever made a run at me. I did encounter bears several times on the trail. Three or four times the bear would rare up, they can see and hear better, I guess when they are up on their hind legs. They would rear up, look and sniff. However, I never had a bear charge me.

Author's Disclaimer. In the mid 1930's bear populations were down in Belly River. However, over the decades, both brown and grizzly bear populations have increased. Be sure to read *Hooked for Good, Hooked for Life: The Passion for Fishing Belly River* and *Hiking Bear Country* for my updated caution and advice on bears.

Never hike alone.

Alas, it is not against Park rules to go skinny-dipping.

CHAPTER 13

TRAPPING THE TRAPPER

Trapper's Paradise — every beaver lodge and pond meant lots of steady income.

The Trapper

Joe Cosley was a mountain man trapper — a dying breed.

When the trapping season started Cosley was as busy as a beaver taking care of business. He made preparations in November, usually for a line of credit, or he would get grub staked by someone. I have no problem with his trapping per say. However, he should not have trapped Glacier Park and Waterton Park or any park.

From studies of his life I have learned that Cosley had a vital interest in the wildlife and had a livable relationship with them.

A hallmark of this man was that he could be out in the wilderness mountains for months at a time by himself, and surprisingly, maintain his sanity. He often told friends how much he enjoyed being alone at times in the mountains. He felt sorry for anyone who couldn't stand to be alone with himself. After seeing Glacier's Belly River Mountains and river system, he was captured for good.

He loved the solitude of the mountains with its lakes and streams and the beauty of nature. He liked the challenge of snowshoeing the pristine snow-covered forests and clearings seeking the elusive marten and mink. Beaver and muskrat were his bread and butter. Cosley also trapped weasel in season — the snow white ermine.

He lived in harmony with the earth and its creatures. But he did not live in harmony with the laws governing national parks. The call of prime marten and beaver country got the best of him, and he lived the life of his choice.

Joe lived alone most of his life. He was a mountain man and a loner. Trapping is more than just making sets. Trapping is understanding the quarry. Cosley had studied the habits of wild animals all his life. He knew how to make sets, tend his trapline, put up his fur and reap the rewards.

I doubt that Cosley was a perfect trapper, catching 100% from every trap he used. I'm sure he had his share of snapped or empty traps. However, his hands-on skills of pelt preparation like combing, wiping, and fleshing were top rate. Fur industry people have said that Cosley's furs always brought top dollar.

He was interested in conservation, the management of wildlife. This is revealed from the fact that his furs were all large adult sizes. He knew how to properly put up his furs. His furs were extra large, prime, well-furred, undamaged, clean skins — the highest grades. He was harvesting a renewable resource. This was renewable resource management at its best. The cycle is clear. Take a few beaver or risk population overruns. Over-crowding leads to disease, and the population sometimes dies off completely. Areas not trapped do not produce as much as areas where there is systematic trapping. He had a trapping program that went without a hitch until Heimes caught him red-handed.

If Cosley had trapped out of the parks perhaps things would have been better for him. Perhaps he would have been more open about his life and his way of life. Alas, he was always secretive about his trapline life — except to brag about how great he was. His cabins and trap camps were well concealed away from everyone. Some say he liked being left alone, but there was more to it than that. He was careful of not being found out or caught.

If we had visited Cosley in his trapline camp we would have found the usual traps, tools and supplies. However, Cosley rarely allowed anyone to visit his camp or see his operating trapline.

Cosley was known to take as many beaver, muskrats, marten, mink and other furbearers with his .22 rifle as he was his traps. He was known as a rimfire fur trapper. He was always a great shot. His war buddies said he was a marksman. Two fur buyers of Cosley's paid premium rates because there was no damage to his pelts. That's the proof of how great a shot Joe was.

Heimes' Briefings about Cosley

The Park told me about Cosley. I had heard about Joe Cosley from the time I was hired. When I was suddenly transferred to Belly River the Park officials updated me on the district. They told me more about Joe Cosley, and that he was probably still operating his trapline in Belly River and in Canada. Reports were being received that Cosley annually bragged of selling prime fur he harvested from Belly River.

Then the Park told me that Waterton Park also suspected Cosley trapping in their park. When Cosley was trapping illegally in Canada that was their problem. When Joe Cosley was trapping and poaching in Belly River, that was my problem. I wanted to solve my problem.

The story of Joe Cosley in Belly River covers a 40 year period from his arrival in the late 1800's (1889). From the time Cosley arrived in Belly River country he trapped and hunted. That includes when he was a ranger there with the Forest Service before it was made Glacier National Park. Cosley was Belly River's first ranger.

After being fired from Glacier, Joe Cosley joined the Canadian Army and fought in World War I. I learned of Cosley's record of killing over a 100 German soldiers. Cosley was a sniper and being a great shot he was able to kill dozens of German snipers. With me being German, that made it even worse. I didn't want to be another German shot by Cosley.

Oh! The stories I have heard about Joe Cosley. He was an educated Indian and at one time was on the lecture tour for two winters. He lectured about Waterton Park and Glacier National Park and the wildlife.

I was told to be on the lookout for Cosley year round. The park had heard recent stories that Cosley was still selling Belly River furs in the Cardston area. Sooner or later, stories like that get back to headquarters.

Early Signs

Looking back, Cosley made three big mistakes when he went into Belly River the winter of 1928 and stayed the spring of 1929.

I saw evidence that he was trapping in there in 1928. He had a partner in there with him then. I caught that fellow in 1928. I was coming back from John J. West's with my mail. It was about 8 o'clock in the evening and about two miles south of the boundary. I was on my horse. I saw some guy moving across the old wagon road, so I punched the horse a little in the sides and caught up. He was on foot and could not outrun a horse. I got off the horse real quick. He had a .22 rifle. He told me some name and said he was from the Cardston area and he was Cosley's partner.

I didn't want to go to headquarters with him. I didn't have time. I took his rifle, emptied his shells out, and gave it back to him and I told him to get across the boundary and *never* come back. "The next time you will not get by so easy." I never saw or heard of him again.

Fresh Signs

Every year we had to dynamite one or two beaver dams that flooded the wagon trail from J. J. West's. We brought in supplies in the spring and again in the fall with team and wagon, so this trail had to be cleared and dry for those shipments.

During the winter months with the dog team and sleigh I would go over the dams if they were frozen or around them when they weren't but I knew that in the spring I had to deal with each dam. I wouldn't blow the dams during the winter months because then the beaver or beaver family could freeze without the protection of the dam and their food supply would be frozen too.

Many reporters have said that I noticed that a beaver dam had flooded the road that came from Canada but this is not true. I and every ranger was aware the dams were there and in the spring needed to be dynamited out to lower the water level and to be dry for the wagon to get through with needed supplies for both the summer and winter.

I have magazines here that have the account. But some of these articles in the magazines have quite a few mistakes in them. I'll tell you more about these mistakes later.

This was now my third spring in the Belly River area. The main part of the story of the capture of Cosley began on Monday morning of May 6th, 1929. Weather was clear and the 7 a.m. temperature was 32°. I wasn't looking for Cosley at that time.

There was a large beaver dam on the east side of the river about a mile from Canada. The water in the dam was blocking the wagon road further east of the dam. The water level would be up to the bed of a wagon. Every spring the beaver would build it up higher. They don't call them "eager beavers" for nothing.

As we always had several loads of stuff coming in with supplies in the spring and again in the fall, *this* was the time to dynamite the dams. After I would blow a dam the water would all go out overnight and the trail would be dry in a few days.

This is where some of the articles got it wrong. I was *not* looking for Joe Cosley at this time.

So I was going down to this area to blow out the beaver dams because we were having some stuff delivered in a week or two. It was 8:30 in the morning. I had the TNT on my horse and I was scouting around to find the best place to put the charges in the dam.

The beaver dam that year was straight. Other years it was curved. I was going along the river and there was a sand patch. Cosley made the mistake of putting his foot in that sand.

Right away I could tell the foot print was really fresh, maybe made that morning. The track was near the edge of the river and pointing at the river to the west. The river was only half a foot deep at the time before high water started.

I wanted to know who else was in the park besides myself, so I followed the foot prints. They meandered around the river, and I lost them but my dog picked them up again. She followed the tracks about a half a mile or so back down the river and all of a sudden she ran into the bush and came out dragging the carcass of a beaver. The hide was off so I knew there was somebody in there trapping beaver. I then figured the person might be out looking after beaver traps.

So then I forgot all about blowing the beaver dams out. I thought, "Well, I'm going to have to cross the river and find out about this foot print." I mounted up and crossed the river, and back in the woods a little ways there was still some snow banks that he couldn't hardly dodge and he left a few more fresh foot prints in there.

I staked the horse on the far north end of the lower flat. I couldn't take the horse through the woods up ahead; the trees were like a hair brush in there. I had one dog with me. Nellie and I followed these tracks.

So I followed these tracks for a mile, losing them several times and the dog had to help me a few times. I came into an open place, a clearing, and Nellie found a carcass of a beaver at the edge of the clearing. We went a little way further and suddenly the dog's ears went up. She stopped on the top of a hill and looking below I saw a camp down there. I saw what looked like a white tent there, it was more a lean-to. This was at 9 a.m.

So I figured I found Cosley's camp but what should I do now? I didn't want to walk right into the camp because I didn't want to leave any sign or nothing there at all. I hid in the bushes so I could see if there was any movement in the camp.

No movement. I stayed there until 3 o'clock in the afternoon and nobody showed up. Well, then I thought, he saw or heard me as I was going down the river.

I decided to go down and scout the camp out carefully. There was a pole on a slope and over it was a white tarp. Inside the tent were lots of pine bows held in place by ground poles on either side. On top of the pine bows was his bedding.

I found a bunch of beaver traps and three muskrat hides between the blankets. I left everything just the way I found it and then I went back to my hiding place. I was beginning to think Cosley had seen me and he wouldn't come back.

So then at 3:15 it was getting chilly and the mosquitoes were biting too. So I thought, "Well, if I am going to have to stay out all night I will go back to the station and get some warmer clothes." I was smoking in those days. I wanted to get something to eat and a new package of cigarettes. I got a more experienced horse, that could be picketed out.

At the station, before I went back to the stakeout, I called up Waterton. At that time I had to go through the Canadian Belly River Station, to Waterton Park Headquarters, to get to the head of the Waterton Lake (Goat Haunt R. S.).

Tom Whitcraft was stationed there. But Tom was one of these womanizers like some of our politicians are today. He liked women. He was a young fellow over six feet tall and dark and handsome. He looked like Clark Gable. He finally married a Canadian girl.

I thought if I called up Tom and told him to come up to Belly River right away, as soon as he could, I would have the backup I needed.

Well, I couldn't get Tom. He wasn't home. He was on the Canadian side for sure. However, Waterton Park could not get him (by phone), so I didn't have a chance to talk to Tom. So I told them at Waterton Park to keep on trying and tell him to be sure and come up to Belly River, and I gave them all the instructions I could: where to cross the river, how far to go back to the north end of that lower flat there west of the hill, and I would leave some extra tracks there pointing the way.

It was clear to me that Waterton Park wanted to cooperate with me to catch Joe Cosley, and they were going to help me. I gave Waterton lots of good instructions, that Tom wouldn't need any snowshoes but he had to cross the river. He needed to come just as soon as he was told.

There was no need to phone Park Headquarters yet.

CHAPTER 14

THE STAKE OUT, BY HEIMES

I went back to the trapper's camp.[68] This time I also packed my coat and a pair of hobbles and rode Old Irish. I turned the horse loose about a mile or two from this camp. I went to a place about 150 feet from this secret camp and hid myself again. By then it was 5 o'clock. I stayed behind some bushes until just before dark. I laid down one time to get some rest but I was worked up and couldn't sleep. My dog was with me but she would not bark.

As the sun went down I thought Cosley must have seen me for sure and had taken off for Canada. It was 8:45 p.m., and I was in the shadow of Sentinel Mountain and it was getting cold.

My Malamute dog was laying beside me. Just as it started to get dark her ears went up — she heard something below. Sure enough, here comes a great big guy moving swiftly, taking big strides.

He had a .22 rifle on his shoulder and he came down another draw from the north into his camp. He put his rifle against the pine tree and went to scratch up some dry grass to start his fire. The rifle was only six feet from his fire pit. He had a pole across the fire where he hung his tea bucket. That pole also had some parts of beaver on it too, smoking them there when he built his fire.

There was only a little moon. By this time it was dusk and I didn't have much daylight left so I waited until Cosley got his fire going a bit.

I slowly started toward the camp. Cosley was stooping down scratching up more grass and twigs. I was about 15 feet away from him when he heard me step on a twig.

---

[68] Said Heimes during a interview with author. Then, over several more sessions he told me the whole story.

He automatically reached for his rifle as he looked my way, but I had my rifle with my finger on the trigger and I hollered at him, "If you put your hand on that gun I'll shoot you right through the guts."

Not taking his eyes off me once, he slowly pulled his hand back and stood up. At that time, I wondered if I had made a mistake. Cosley was head and shoulders taller than I was. He was big.

I had never seen Joe Cosley or even a picture of him, but I had a hunch. And there was my logic: Belly River + foot prints near beaver dam + beaver carcass stripped of pelt = Joe Cosley.

I asked him what his name was. He didn't say Joe Cosley. He said Jack Robertson or some thing. I had a few descriptions of him, and he fit those so I told him, "You look more like Joe Cosley to me. You are under arrest."

Well, then, he figured I knew him so he said, "Yes, I'm Joe Cosley all right, but there is *no* ranger in the park taking me in."

That was his third big mistake.

His first big mistake was coming into the park knowing that I had caught his partner the year before. His second big mistake was that first footprint in the sand. His biggest mistake was when he said, "There is *no* ranger in this park taking me in."

I didn't have any other choice then. I might have let him go. I did not want to go to headquarters. However, with Cosley's challenge I had to take him in. I could not have lived with myself for the rest of my life.

By now, it was too dark to take him a half mile through the thick woods to the clearing by myself. There was no trail or nothing. I not only had my pistol and his rifle and knife; I had seven of his steel traps, some parts of beaver and muskrat hides. And I had Cosley to handle.

I was pretty well loaded down. By the time I put that pack sack on my back I was in no condition to fight in a hurry so I decided I was not going through a half mile of thick woods in the dark with this guy. It would be bad enough in the daytime. I saw Cosley had enough wood stacked against a tree to keep the fire going all night.

So all night long we sat by the fire. I kept throwing wood on just to keep a little light around there. He even complained about me burning all his firewood. Imagine. Here was Cosley who entered the USA illegally, I had arrested him for trapping and poaching in Glacier Park, and he had the nerve to complain about me using up his firewood to keep the fire going and get enough light so Cosley could not escape from me.

He kept coming up with reasons he had to leave the camp. Three times, I had to go with him to take a leak. He didn't have to go that much but he figured that it was maybe a good chance for him to get away.

But I stayed so close to him with my gun pointed at him that he didn't try to run for it.

It was some time before I realized that Cosley talked with a quiet soft voice. Several times, I had to ask him to repeat himself before I heard him. After that, I started to really listen to each quiet word in order to understand him. The voice and the man didn't seem to go together. Big tough man. Quiet voice.

He chewed the rag all the time and tried to get me to turn him loose. It hurt his pride a little bit to be caught, perhaps even more so by such a young kid as me. In addition, he had been trapping in the park for so long (40 years) and he didn't want to come in now or ever.

Cosley was starting to realize that I was not going to leave him alone long enough to get loose. About 12:30, Cosley suggested that there was enough room in his bunk for the two of us; we might as well get some sleep. I wondered if he thought if I was ignorant enough to go to bed with him. He said, "Well, there is no use in us losing any sleep over this."

I don't need any sleep. I told him that I'll keep the fire going and be right here guarding him. So he didn't go to bed either.

Later Joe told me that he saw me on the other side of the river that morning riding my horse, but he thought I was going to Mountain View for my mail. We talked about many things that night. He was more relaxed now.

Joe also said he watched me at the station and he knew what time I went to bed at night and got up in the mornings. He knew my routine. I wondered what the hell he wanted to do that for. If it was true that Cosley spied on me, I wondered why one of my dogs didn't bark.

Joe Cosley seemed to know a lot about H. C. Hockett and me but I did not know much about Cosley. What was Cosley thinking about to spy on me? The only reason I came up with was that Cosley knew he was poaching and trapping illegally, but he still wanted to trap and poach so he became a sneak and lived a secret life.

The conversation varied between what great things Cosley said he had done and ways he tried to bribe me to let him go. I just let him talk to pass the time until dawn came.

He told me that when J. J. West arranged with Duke Sanders to take my shipment and me into Belly River in December 1926, Cosley was staying with Duke. Cosley talked as if he knew many ranchers in Alberta, and maybe he did.

To finish the story, Cosley said he planned to wait at Duke's ranch until Duke and his son returned the next day. However, they returned late that same night. After they all got the horses cared for, Duke and Cosley laughed all night talking about how young the new kid ranger was. Their guess was that I would last a week and either be dead or would run home to mama. Cosley said Duke was proven wrong.

I started to realize just how popular this Cosley really might be to some of those Canadian ranchers. I was worried one of those friends might come up here to drop in to visit Cosley and see that I was there. I didn't like even the chance of it, see.

He said he was born in Ontario to a French Canadian trapper and a Cree Indian mother on the Seven Nations Indian Reserve. He grew up in this wealthy home and attended college. He then moved to Montana and the Northwest Territories (that was what Alberta was called before Canada made it the Province of Alberta in 1905). He said he lectured about Glacier and Waterton Parks and wildlife for years.

I had heard about the lecturing part before; however, I replied that I had heard that he was from the Chippewa Tribe, and he changed his mind and agreed. Then I told him I had also heard that he was also Algonquin. Which was it Cosley, I asked him? Chippewan he replied. That worried me the most because I understood that the Chippewa were fierce fighters, ready to pick a fight to the bloody death for no apparent reason other than just the opportunity to fight.

Cosley had lots to say all night. I never stopped him. He asked about Hockett. Cosley liked Hockett because old man Hockett was never in the park much and if he was, 'he sure liked his apple jack.'

Cosley said he had never seen Hockett sober. He told me he ran into Hockett on the trail one time and warned Hockett to never set foot on that trail again. It seemed to work because Cosley never saw or heard Hockett coming down the trail again. Hockett spent most of his days after that in Canada where he could get his liquor.

I told Cosley that I had heard that Ralph Thayer had been sent by Glacier National Park to go to Belly River and find Cosley and put the fear of god into Cosley, back in the late spring of 1914. I further told Cosley that I was aware he was fired and that there would be no more paychecks after that. And Ralph was to also tell Joe Cosley to never come back to Glacier. Cosley didn't talk about it and he was silent for a long time.

We knew a lot of the same people, and we talked about most of them with me standing holding a gun on Cosley and him sitting on his bedroll. But Cosley seemed to know some of the old timers that I didn't. He said that some of them would be upset when they found out that I had arrested him. He said he had lots of friends on both sides of the border.

I told him I thought he would have got the message last year when, "I caught your pardner in here working for you. That should have been a warning to you. You made a mistake in coming back this year." He admitted that so-and-so did work for him, but quit without notice or even talking to Cosley and he never heard anymore from his pardner.

I informed him that I did not think that was true because this .22 caliber rifle looks just like the one pardner had last year, scratch and all. How did you get it back and not talk to pardner? Cosley was silent for some time after that question. It was the only rest my ears got.

We just looked at each other for a long time. Cosley eventually reached for a beaver part and tore off a piece for himself and started chewing. The meal and the silence was short lived.

The bribes started. He said he had several cabins in Southern Alberta, and he wanted me to take one of them and let him go. What would I do with a cabin in a place I didn't want to be? Was I to sell the cabin or move it? If there was such a cabin, did Cosley really own it? I don't think so.

Cosley was not sensible in some things. Joe Cosley was shooting the breeze and I just let him. The fact was that Cosley was arrested and I was taking him in and that was final.

He recalled he fought a Sioux Indian and although Cosley was stabbed several times, he won the fight and he killed the Sioux Indian. Cosley continued that after all these years he still had the large scars all over his back from the knife wounds received from that Indian fight.

He said he arrived in Great Falls, Montana in 1887 and Kalispell in 1889 and had trapped in Glacier and Waterton ever since. That would have been for 40 years.

He said he worked for the Forest Service, on and off, until he joined Glacier Park. He said he worked on Ahern pass with Lieutenant George Ahern and his detachment in 1890. Ahern Pass was used in the summer months back in those early days.

Cosley told me he was a famous marksman and horseman in Buffalo Bill's Wild West Show,[69] went to London, and Paris and all over America. He also said he was a sharp shooter in the war (WW1). I had heard the last part but had no way to know if either were true.

He admitted he trapped fur in Glacier and Waterton Parks since 1889 and the price for good fur was higher in Canada. He wanted me to

---

[69] It may be true but Cosley would have been very young. According to the records there was no Colsey fancy rider or fancy shooter on any Bill Cody roster. Also, when the Wild West Show was in Paris, Cosley was in Ontario, Canada. Maybe it is just another Cosley story.

start working for him. I told him I was working for the Park and was not going to work for him.

Continuing his thought, Cosley replied that I could stay working for the Park but trap on the side. That way I could keep the Park from finding out what I was doing with the trapping. I told him again that I was working for the Park to protect against poaching, and trapping, that he was under arrest, would be taken in and tried and found guilty, and put in jail for a long time.

The talk of jail time got him for awhile.

He talked of the early days in the park and at the Belly River Ranger Station, about Park Head Quarters brass. He said he loved Belly River because it was so beautiful and untouched in lakes and streams and valley but the best part was that Head Quarters people never came there. I agreed with all points. He continued that Belly River was some of the most scenic in the country, and that he could travel at will from one country to the other without being stopped or checked by anyone.

I reminded him the Canadian Wardens were looking for him too and if they ever caught him he would be arrested and jailed for a long time in Canada. He thought highly of the Canadian Parks people but then he wasn't getting paid by them while trapping like he did in Glacier Park.

I suggested that when he got out of jail in Montana he could be re-arrested and taken into Canada and taken to trial there. So you will be among those you would like to be with—Canadian prison guards.

Cosley didn't like my determination that he was going in. He told me what Ralph Thayer had told him when Ralph came in to get Cosley out and told Cosley to never come back. Cosley didn't like Ralph after that. Cosley would not want to meet Ralph again. That's when Cosley found he could kill two birds by joining the Canadian Army to fight in W.W.I.

From time to time Cosley would mention or ask about another old timer. I knew most of them. Some, I think, had already died. The name of a Lake McDonald old timer named Howe came up, but I can't remember his first name right now. Maybe it was Charlie Howe.

Cosley was a talker that night. After he knew I was not going to be going to sleep he seemed to want to talk. He relaxed a bit and talked. At one time he talked so much I thought he was trying to talk me to death. In looking back I think he told me things because he thought he would get away from me sometime in the night or first thing in the morning, and then it wouldn't matter what I knew about him.

We talked about odds and ends.

He said he trapped several marten this season as well as mink. Of course, all his trapping was done on the Canadian side. So I asked him what he was doing on this side with muskrat hides under his bedroll, beaver parts all around his camp and these traps? He didn't answer me, just changed the subject.

I didn't know what to believe because he said things that I knew were just not true and the others were probably bull shit too. It did pass the time on what turned out to be my longest night ever.

He told me he knew my complete patrol routine — where I would be each day. He even suggested that when I was in Mountain View or over Gable Pass going around Chief he often used his 22 rifle rather than to trap. If I wasn't gone from the valley Cosley would use his knife to kill a trapped animal rather than risk the rifle shot being heard.

Well, I never did hear rifle shots, but what was I to believe with all these stories.

He remembered the early days prospecting and mining in Glacier. One highlight that he mentioned twice was knowing Kootenai Brown. He raved about Brown and his wife's cooking. He said that Kootenai Brown liked the fancy way Cosley dressed; that Brown copied Cosley's style of dress. I think it was the other way around.

He told me he rarely used the wagon trail to the Ranger Station because it was the heaviest traveled of all. Cosley liked to stay in the trees and would sometimes hike the Lee Ridge and then descend Gable Mountain and still beat others looking for him. Cosley said he didn't like to meet those that he did not know well, and so he stayed out of sight.

I think he stayed out of sight because he did not want to be caught with his rifle, traps, pelts and the animal parts he cooked and ate.

Joe Cosley recounted a time when Norman Pearl and Cy Bellah came to check up on him. They went all the way to the Ranger Station and couldn't find Cosley. He said he was so close to them that he overheard them talking about him, accusing him that he was not even in Belly River. Cosley said he sometimes shadowed park visitors but was never seen by any.

The stars were bright that night, first in awhile. Belly River is so far from any city or town. Sometimes I tuned Cosley out, and just let him talk and talk. I wondered to myself how any person had so much to say. No golden silence tonight.

He told me why he named the lakes Helen, Elizabeth, Sue and Margaret Lakes. Sue was the coldest. Elizabeth his best. He wasn't talking about the temperature of the lakes. He said he had lots of lady friends. But he was a bachelor like me so what was so special about him. He said he wrote poems for them and brought them flowers. I don't do poetry.

For years every map and every person called the east lake on the middle fork or west fork (Mokowanis River) “Crossley” or “Crosley.” No one knew how it got spelled that way. But at the time I caught Joe Cosley that night we talked of it, and he said it was spelled wrong on the maps from Washington D.C.

I think it is good that Crossley Lake has finally been changed to Cosley Lake and also the mountain to Cosley Ridge. Although it really isn’t a ridge, you know. It is a mountain.

I was tired, but my mind was racing about how I was going to get Cosley out of there through those trees and back to my horse. At times I just half listened to Cosley carry on about what he did and how great he was to himself so I could plan a way to get him out.

I was thinking to myself about different situations that might happen in the morning when it was time to get Cosley away from his camp and back to the Ranger Station. Once there, I could phone and make arrangements to bring Cosley in to trial. I was hoping I could just drive him out through Canada.

With me being younger than him (Cosley was 58 and I was 24) I knew that if he started to run I would have it over him. Before I came to the park I played football for three years in an athletic club. I was good at running and tackling.

He did everything he could think of to talk me into letting him go. He told me he would show me where there was a big cave in the park that nobody knew about except him. It would be a big scenic attraction for Glacier Park, and I would be famous for telling the park about it. He offered to show me where that cave was.

He also had a gold watch. I don’t think he had it with him though. I don’t know if the chain was gold or not. He offered to give me that gold watch if I turned him loose. He said the watch was worth $150 and so valuable that after I turned him loose and he got back to Canada, he would buy it back from me for $100. He said I couldn’t lose out.

If I turned him loose how would I know if he would later show me where the cave was or if I turn him loose how do I know if he would give me the watch? All empty words and logic but I let him talk. Cosley was under my arrest.

Then he wanted me to be his partner again. I told him he was the one under arrest, and he would soon be at park headquarters and put on trial for trapping and poaching in Glacier. Then he would be in jail.

The words were still burning in my ears, “There is *no* ranger in this park that’s taking me in.” There would be no letting him go!

Towards first light I had smoked just about all my cigarettes. I had smoked about a whole pack of cigarettes that night. That was the toughest night I ever spent in my life. However, I could not let sleep overtake me or he would be gone, probably shooting me dead on his way.

Along toward morning Joe asked me what I would do if he didn't go in the morning. I told him I would cut me a switch and "I will beat you all the way to the Ranger Station." He kind of laughed. I still did not know what I would do in the morning. I did cut the stick.

Well he finally got it in his head that I was not going to let him go.

When I was down to my last cigarette, I told him, "When this cigarette is gone, we've got to go because I'm out of cigarettes." When that cigarette was about half-gone Cosley said, "Okay, I'll go along."

I told him to gather up whatever he wanted to take with him and we leave as soon as it gets a little lighter. He did pick up a small packsack. Besides all the other stuff, I had a stick to carry too. I wish I had a picture of me carrying all that stuff.

Well at first light, it was time to leave Cosley's concealed camp and take him back to where I had Old Irish staked out. Cosley had nothing to carry but his small packsack of clothes, and I had a pack full of heavy evidence and the three guns.

In addition, Cosley knew the area like his own hand.

It was hard to get Cosley going in the morning. He was a hard guy to get going against his will. He wanted to go the other way, north into Canada.

It was 7 a.m. when Joe was finally ready to go. We only went about 300 feet and he broke away and just left the country all at once and took off running. He never even told me he was leaving.

I had to slip my packsack off real quick, drop my guns, and take after him. I chased and caught him in about a hundred feet or so. I was a lot faster going through the woods than he was. I brought him down with a flying tackle. We scuffled a few minutes.

Well, after I held him there for a while, he said he would go and not make any more trouble. We went about another 200 feet and he broke away again, this time going over 500 feet before I caught him again. I shoved him down in the brush on his stomach and sat on him. He said that if I got off him he would go.

Well then, I figured if I was going to have to do this all the way back to the station, I might as well tie him up, get my horse, and pack him out.

He promised again even more sincerely that he would go without trouble. He said he was now sick and couldn't run any more. I did not believe him and I tied his feet.

After that he promised to go if I untied his feet. After several minutes I did untie him.

We went about 500 more feet under control and this time he turned around, looking me right in the eyes he shouted, “This is as far as I am going. You can go back to the station. I am going north from here.” We started fighting. He took a swing at me and got me good. I still had the backpack on.

He wasn’t trying to kill me I don’t think — but just to get away. But I was better at fighting than he was. I did quite a bit of amateur boxing in California before I came to Glacier Park. I told him he was going right along with me and I grabbed hold of him to turn him around and get him started.

The trees were thick like a hair brush. Too many trees around. You couldn’t take a hay-maker swing or anything. Didn’t have much room to fight decent, see.

He scuffed with me and just about got away from me.

But all of sudden I got his head against a tree and I saw my chance to bump his head against the tree. I took a piece of hide off my hands from the bark on the trees and that gave me a lot of trouble for several weeks later. My hand was infected for weeks.

So then he dropped down like a log. He might have been out for a few seconds but not very long because then he started to talk a little. He was down on his belly again and this time I was sitting on him. I would like to have a picture of that.

He said, “I’m sick. I can’t go.”

I said, “That’s good. I hope you get sicker because maybe you will come along a lot better if you get good and sick. If you get really sick I can always go out and get the horse and tow you out.”

So there I was sitting on Cosley in the woods there and Cosley said he was sick. If I was Cosley I would be sick too. While I was resting sitting on top of Cosley, I look at my watch and the time was 7:58. I had been running all over hell for an hour trying to get Cosley to come in under arrest.

My dog was laying along side there. She was wondering what this was all about.

But then, all of a sudden her ears went up and she was looking back towards the trail the way I came in, and she could hear there was somebody coming through the trees and snow.

I first saw one guy coming towards us about 150 yards away. Gee, I thought I was in for it. This may be Cosley’s partner coming back in. I didn’t have my pistol or rifle. So I got up and stood behind a tree and kept watching for any sign through the trees.

Then I saw a second person in front of the first guy. I knew I was in trouble now. But then I noticed a sheep skin sports cap from L. L. Bean that the Glacier Park people use to wear. As soon I saw that I hollered at them. It was Tom Whitcraft and the Canadian Warden, Bert Barnes. These guys were trying to pick up my trail, you see. They had had quite a time finding their way in as there was no trail.

Tom had finally got the message after he got back from chasing his girl friend. He came up on horse from Bert Barnes' at the Canadian Station on the Belly River in Alberta. Tom didn't even go back to the Goat Haunt Station. He had stopped at Waterton and someone told him I wanted to see him in Belly River. So he came right in there that morning. He was out with this girl until 2 in the morning and the rest was traveling time to Belly River and breakfast on the Canadian side.

Bert had horses there and so they came up on horses. They crossed the river and followed my tracks and saw my horse in the clearing so they left their horses there too. They picked up my trail on foot where I left my tracks in the snow in the forest pointing the way I went.

Tom said I sure left good instructions and directions on how to get here. He said he was sorry he was late.

Bert Barnes came up with him so I had plenty of help when they arrived. As soon as these men showed up this bird wasn't sick any more. So while Tom and Bert and I were talking Cosley slowly gets up and he wasn't sick any more then. He saw there was no use playing opossum any more because there were three of us to the one of him.

I went back to Cosley's camp while Tom watched him and I got some more things as evidence.

So most of my bad problems were over. I tied Cosley's hands up and we rounded up all my gear, pack, guns, traps and other evidence and headed to where the horses were. I tied a rope to Cosley and he walked.

When I got back at the river, I picked up some more of Cosley's traps which I had found the second time into his camp. Tom and I took the prisoner

When we got across the river Bert Barnes said he might as well go back across the line so he turned left and went home down the old wagon trail. Tom and I and Cosley and my dog turned right and headed south to the Ranger Station.

What a long night.

"The weather was clear and the day was starting to warm up. On the way back I spotted more beaver signs. Tom and I talked all the way to the station. Cosley didn't say a word." ended Heimes.

But the day was only starting.

Heimes had his work cut out for him

Glacier National Park old headquarters in 1929.
The telephone operators worked upstairs.

CHAPTER 15

HEIMES MAKING ARRANGEMENTS

Belly River Station Calling [70]

"I was soon to realize just how much work there was regarding the capture of Joe Cosley, the Indian Poacher," started off Heimes.

Before we arrived at the Ranger Station I could hear my dogs. They were hungry. I knew I would have to feed them right away.

When we got Cosley tied up at the station Tom said, "Well, I guess you won't need me any more."

I knew I had to talk to Tom. I said, "You are going all the way to headquarters with me because if I get into any more trouble with Cosley and it is known that you were here with me and you wanted to go back to your station, and your girl friend, you'll get your ass in a sling." Which he would have.

So Tom reluctantly decided to join me all the way.

I told Tom to cook something up for us to eat while I went to feed the dogs and check on the horses.

After acting so sick and dying Cosley was ready to eat. As we ate I gave Tom a list of things to do after he washed the dishes: where to find my second pair of snowshoes, to take Cosley to the outhouse and look after him and make sure he doesn't get away. I told Cosley that if he got away I would get him good.

Tom asked what I would be doing and I told him I was going to make some phone calls including the most famous phone call the Park headquarters had ever received.

---

[70] Interviews with Joe Heimes between 1989 and 1993

I first called up a fellow by the name of Andy Ford.[71] He was at Waterton. He was the Royal Canadian Mounted Police at Waterton Park. I called him to see about taking Cosley out through[72] Canada by way of John J. West's, to Mountain View and Cardston and back into Montana at Carway / Port of Piegan.

Andy said, "No you can't do that because the minute Cosley crosses that line into Canada he is a free man. You don't have any jurisdiction in Canada." Andy went on to tell me that if I did force Cosley to go with me via Canada he could have pressed charges against me for kidnapping him at force and I would be in deep trouble. Even though it would have been a lot easier to take Cosley through Canada, and Canada wanted to catch Cosley just like we did, that's the law on jurisdiction: crooks break the law anyway they want to but the law has to obey the law in arresting and transporting them to trial and justice.

So there was nothing else to do but to take him over Gable Pass. I was not going to take Cosley over Ahern Pass. Never.

So then I had to call park headquarters up. Our only contact with the outside world was the phone and that system went through Canada.

I called the Canadian Belly River Station, to Waterton Park, to Mountain View, to Cardston, to Lethbridge, to Shelby Montana, to Browning, to East Glacier, to Belton, and finally to the Park. That was quite a job just getting a hold of headquarters. And there was probably more than eight operators listening in on that famous phone call.

We weren't supposed to make calls to headquarters. However, maybe this situation would be an exception.

When I finally got through to headquarters and told them what the conditions were, and that there was a fellow we wanted to bring all the way into headquarters. Boy, were they tickled when they heard it was Joe Cosley. The Park operator put my call right through.

So after so many years of trying to get him and so many years of Cosley laughing in the Park's face every time he sold his furs — it was a great moment for them. I wish I had a picture of the Park headquarters

---

[71] Corporal Andrew (Andy) Ford was the best hand-gun shot in the R.C.M.P. and Frank Goble' Scoutmaster for several years.

[72] There might have been a way Heimes could have taken Cosley out through Canada and back into Montana again. If Cosley had been tried, found guilty, sentenced and needed to be moved to another jail via Canada, the US government could petition the Canadian government to obtain permission to so transport the prisoner through Canada. However, this whole process could take months and there was no way of a trial for Cosley without taking him first to Belton, Montana.

people after they heard Cosley was coming in. They were jumping for joy, and were so excited on the phone they were shouting.

I told headquarters the best way to bring Cosley out would be to have someone from Glacier Park (East Glacier) come up to Babb in a car and drive up towards Slide Lake on the north side of Kennedy Creek (Otatso Creek) on the south side of Old Chief Mountain. They could come up to Slide Lake as far as they could get. They could only get to about one mile east of the park boundary with Blackfeet Indian Reserve.

I was told to stay on the phone, and I waited with that thing glued to my ear for hours. Every now and then someone came on the line and asked a question or told me what they were trying to do and who they were trying to contact and arrange things with. That was a very long "long-distance" phone bill, I am sure.

It was arranged that Louis "Lou" O. Hanson, Assistant Chief Ranger would come in his "government model" Model T Ford to meet us there at Slide Lake the next day and we would hike down Gable Pass and meet him at the Patrol Cabin or Roberts Ranch just out of the park.

The Park was making arrangement to have a Commissioner there and it looked like it would be scheduled for sometime on Friday. Tom and I would have to stay until after the trial.

The arrangements were confirmed.

I had chores to do and it was getting dark when I finished.

One meal cooked by Tom was enough for me. I made supper but had Tom clean up. All three of us agreed that my cooking was the best.

I let Cosley sleep in my bedroom that night but I locked him up inside pretty good.. If Cosley tried to get out of the window it would make a lot of noise and he would be in deeper trouble. And I told him so. Tom Whitcraft and I took turns sleeping on the bed in the living room and watching. Cosley got a good night sleep in my bedroom.

I took the first watch and Tom slept. He is one of these guys that *nothing* is going to stop him from getting his sleep.

While Tom slept I wrote some reports and made a list to call Bert in the morning. I woke Tom at 2:00 a.m. I had to keep shaking him to get him to wake up.

The previous night was the worst night in my life.

This night at the station wasn't good either. I was too nervous and worked up to sleep. My mind was racing. And I was worried that Tom would fall asleep during his watch. I kept thinking of tomorrow's trail ahead of us and the job to get Cosley over Gable Pass.

The wind was starting to pick up outside. I called out to Tom twice before he answered me. Tom said he couldn't hear me the first time because of the wind that had started. I felt he didn't hear me because he was asleep.

I kept reliving the day's events and that I should have had Cosley carry the heavy evidence in his backpack and I just carry the guns.

I didn't sleep but I did rest. I needed that rest.

"What a way to take Cosley in for trial," remarked Heimes.

Frank Goble has, "long been of the opinion that there was a great deal of prejudice on the part of the Glacier Park Rangers and staff regarding Joe Cosley. They, at that time, referred to him as 'that damned Indian.'" Goble points out from experience that the Canadians were much more tolerant than the Americans towards Indians and liked Joe Cosley. "Wallace Gladstone, also a half-breed, was at that time a Warden in Waterton Park. His brothers Jack and Harry, worked in Waterton Park for most of their working lives. There was also a Dave Tourond, a half-breed, who spent most of his life in Waterton. Bert Barnes was an exception -- he didn't like Cosley.

CHAPTER 16

HIKING TO TRIAL, As Told by Heimes

WEDNESDAY MAY 8

Weather stormy. 7 a.m. temperature is 34°

The next morning the three of us got ready. Nobody but a backcountry ranger would know of all the things that need to be done before you take such a trip as this.

This was the first time Cosley had seen the new station. He said he really liked it. He was even offered to volunteer to help with the chores around the station.

I couldn't have that. He might have got away from us.

Tom did breakfast for us while I did the chores. While Tom cleaned up I phoned Bert Barnes and asked him to come in and feed my dogs, instructed him where everything was and what needed to be done.

With everything arranged we were ready.

Cosley was more cooperative this morning. He even helped Tom adjust the harnesses on the snowshoes Tom was to wear.

The three of us headed east up the trail. There was nothing else to do but to take Cosley over Gable Pass between Gable Mountain and Chief Mountain and down toward Otatso Creek and past Slide Lake to the Slide Patrol Cabin. From there we were to hike to the Park vehicle and drive into Babb and on to East Glacier.

At Gable trailhead, just a short distance from the station, we hit the snow line. I only had two pair of snowshoes at the Station. Tom wore the first pair, my pair, and he took the lead. He also took the muskrat hides and some of the traps.

The wind was picking up. I knew what it would be like on top of Old Gable Mountain and I wasn't looking forward to it.

Cosley wore the second pair of snowshoes and I put him in the middle. I packed some of the traps and beaver parts in his back sack. I was learning.

I was traveling light. I had my pistol and Cosley's rifle.

I followed up in the rear with a rope tied to Cosley. Because I was smaller and lighter I was still able to walk over the mostly compacted snow and only occasionally fell through.

I soon realized that I didn't have to worry about getting Cosley over Gable. It was Tom I had to worry about.

Cosley had been over Gable Pass many times but he was not helping Tom find the way. Tom had never been over Gable Pass and Tom didn't do well on snowshoes.

As I followed up the rear, I could tell Tom was having trouble going up the slope. He stopped several times to catch his breath. It was more than stops to rest—it was his legs. It takes different muscles to snowshoe than walking along a trail or riding a horse. Tom later complained he had charley-horses and sore leg muscles for days after crossing Gable Mountain Trail.

I didn't pay that much attention to how Cosley was doing going up hill until later. Looking back, Cosley never needed to rest and was in better shape than I was.

Gable Pass with snowshoes

Tom needed to rest several times which brought a smile to Cosley. It was the only time I ever saw Joe Cosley smile.

I had to holler to Tom every once in a while on which way to go. Tom wasn't that good on snowshoes going up hill but we finally made the summit.

It is usually windy up on Gable Pass. There is that long stretch of open, wind-swept ridge about two miles long. With no tree cover on top it was very windy on this trip, and I really had to shout to Tom to be heard. Tom complained how cold it was on top.

Sometimes I had to throw a chunk of snow at Tom to get his attention for him to turn around and wait for me to huddle with him and point the way. The west wind literally blew us over several times.

Tom couldn't stay on the trail on top of Gable. He said he couldn't see any tracks in the snow. He may have suffered a degree of white-out. Snow has different whiteness' and you need to see the shadows that snowshoe tracks make, see.

Tom behaved like he was disoriented on top of baldy Gable.

"So we three went on down to Slide Lake a mile below. As soon as we entered the tree line the wind and noise lessened so we could talk and be heard again.

Tom did better going down hill but he sometimes needed to rest. After we arrived at Slide Lake it was another mile east to the Ranger Station. There was a permanent Ranger Station there in the winter time in those days.

I recalled later that Cosley was never out of breath. I believed he could have given me a run for the money on snowshoes. We all had just finished coming over Gable Pass. Cosley was 58 years old but he wasn't over the hill.[73] He had endurance.

This was the slowest trip from Belly River that I have ever taken. We were two hours late.

Channing Powell was there and was aware we were coming. He had been told to stay put at the station. We stopped there and had some cookies and coffee. Lou Hanson met us there. We said our good-byes to Channing and walked the two miles to Lou Hanson's[74] Model T car, then he drove us 45 miles as far as Glacier Park (East Glacier) that night. We were all to stay at Park Quarters at East Glacier.

---

[73] This was two and a half weeks before his 59th birthday.

[74] Goble states that Lou Hanson had been in the Klondike and he came out with $10,000.00 in gold. In the early 1930's Lou was stationed at Goat Haunt and Goble stayed at the cabin with Lou's young assistant for two weeks while Lou was out on a holiday, a stay Goble thoroughly enjoyed.

Map of Cosley Secret Camp

MAP LEGEND

1. 49° 00' 00" North
2. Waterton Lakes National Park
3. International Boundary
4. Glacier National Park
5. Old wagon road
6. Heimes stopped Cosley's trapping partner, 1928
7. Beaver dam fed by two streamlets flooding a large length of the road
8. Fresh foot print in sand
9. Cosley's Secret Camp
10. Foot and horse trail to North Fork Belly River and Miche Wabun Lake

Lou had updates for us on what was scheduled to take place. I wish he had told me separately and not told Cosley about it too.

The closer we got to East Glacier the sicker Cosley said he was. Cosley was locked up in a room with a tray of food and got a good night's sleep. Lou gave me a list of things I had to do like reports to finish writing and details to work out with him. Tom was long asleep before I started my paper work.

Another long day behind us. I turned in to get some sleep.

THURSDAY, MAY 9

Weather stormy. Glacier Park to Belton via train, distance 55 miles.
Tom Whitcraft, Joe Cosley and myself making the trip.

I slept for the first time in really days. Tom had to shake *me*. When I woke I thought he was Cosley trying to kill me and was ready to take his head off.

Then I went to let Cosley out of his locked-up room.

Now, Cosley became *instantly* ill, said he was even sicker than before and would not be able to travel. I told him he was going in all the way and I was going with him and so was Tom and there was *not* going to be any funny business this day.

Then I smiled and said excitedly, 'This is your trial day,' as if it was a day to look forward to. I was anxious to get Cosley delivered to trial and off my hands.

The Train To Belton

After breakfast we took the early morning train from East Glacier to Belton.

When we arrived at the Midvale train station, there was a crowd gathered to see the famous Cosley. For awhile I thought I was a famous person. I thought all these people had traveled some distance just to see me but I was wrong. Cosley was the attraction.

How does word about Joe Cosley get all the way from Belly River to East Glacier.

Tom Whitcraft wanted to returned to Waterton and it wasn't to get back to his job. Lou Hanson insisted that Tom go with me and that he may have to testify. Lou had to stay and do office work and reports.

The three of us boarded the train. The train was packed, and everyone seemed to be talking and looking at us. I guess it was really Cosley they were looking at. I wish I had a picture of all those people looking at Cosley in our custody.

What a long, slow train. Just before we passed Nyack Ranger Station, the train whistled its usual long shrill blast. I was glad I wasn't at Nyack any more.

We arrived at Belton in the middle of the morning. A newspaper reporter was there to meet Cosley, and he took his picture. There was a story in that paper, and I understand other newspapers also carried some of the story of Joe Cosley's arrest and Belton trial.

Things were buzzing.

The Park had accommodations for us. Cosley was locked up until the trial tomorrow. Cosley was put under $500 bond by Commissioner Lindsey at Belton.

I reported to the superintendent what Cosley had told me about this Duke Sanders fellow, and the Park's concern was just how many other Canadians were friends of Cosley. It is a different country you know. The park said that they had heard some other things that they were going to pass on to Washington, and my information would be included.

But then I was soon to discover just how many friends Cosley had all over the Belton area.

CHAPTER 17

THE TRIAL OF THE CENTURY as told by Heimes

FRIDAY, MAY 10
At Belton. Weather clear.

Trial Day

The trial was going to be held at 10 o'clock. I had reports to fill out and stuff to do before the trial. Cosley was locked up and I had my work cut out for me. The U. S. Commissioner reviewed with me in the morning what was going to happen in the trial and for me to be brief and to the point with my report.

At the trial, I was asked to give my account of what happened, show just the evidence and then was dismissed to leave. The trial continued and the verdict came after I left.

* * *

After I testified and was dismissed I got some help putting a new bandage on my sore hand while I visited with the Park's people for awhile. They were more excited about the capture of Joseph Clarence Cosley. They were jumping and talking and kept asking me questions. I answered each but the questions were out of sequence. What a trip. I was glad it was all over. It seemed every park employee was eating over at the Mess Hall. Everybody stayed and asked Tom and I questions. Then I had to get my report written up.

A secretary was assigned to write down my experience and get it all straight from the horses mouth and then type it all up for Park Records. She showed me what she typed and there were several mistakes, not spelling, but facts. So I told her the details and the order of what happened and where it took place. Even though she wanted the short version, it still took all afternoon. I had to go.

The talk on the street was all about Cosley being captured by some ranger. I heard people everywhere talking about it. Most came up to me and asked me questions. They were all friendly. It was the number one topic all over these parts.

I needed a break. I went to the Belton Mercantile. I could believe how loud the train whistle is in Belton. The last east bound train was just chugging out of the station.

When I went into the Merc I ran into one of the owners, a fellow by the name of Mark Sibley. He asked me, "Do you know where Joe Cosley is?" I told him I didn't know where Cosley is. I don't give a damn where he is, just so long as I don't run into him. My hand was still hurting. I had all I wanted of him, and I was glad he was in trial and locked up."

"Well," Sibley said slowly, "Joe Cosley is on his way back into the Belly River right now," lifting his left eyebrow as to tell me he knew something I didn't. There was a chuckle and smiles from the others all around that room. They all thought Cosley had pulled a fast one on us.

It turns out that Mark Sibley did know something that I didn't.

Mark and Martin Sibley and Charlie Howe were aware that Cosley was arrested for poaching in the Park days before the train arrived in Belton with Cosley and Tom and I. They had even arranged to talk to Cosley when he was locked up and were able to pick up Cosley's packsack. I still don't know how that happened.

Then, right after the trial, Charlie[75] got to visit Cosley in person. Charlie returned to the Merc and told Mark the details. They formulated a new faster plan. Mark took $50 out of the cash register to match Charlie's $50. Charlie took the money and paid the bail and brought Cosley back to the store just before noon.

It didn't take Charlie and Mark and other friends long to put the plan into action. Mark supplied a new pair of snowshoes. Charlie was to take Cosley home to get the lunch that Maggie Howe[76] had made and pack up Joe's packsack containing his coat and hiking gear, (she also prepared a trail lunch for Joe), then drive Cosley as far as he could.

---

[75] Holterman, op. cit. Charlie Howe was an early homesteader to Apgar in 1893. Charlie had been a boatman on the Great Lakes and became one of the most expert boatman on Lake McDonald and the Flathead river. Howe Creek, Howe Lake, and Howe Ridge were named after Charlie.

[76] Holterman, op. cit. Maggie was a fine cook and Joe Cosley often visited the Howes at Lake McDonald.

Cosley was going to be eating the special meal Maggie had prepared just for Joe while Charlie Howe drove the car.

At 1 o'clock Cosley could have been out of the car and on his way up and over Ahern Pass and back into Belly River. Imagine that!. An hour or so after his trial ended Cosley had been released, had been provisioned to be on his way on foot heading to Belly River to retrieve his cache of furs.

Why was Mark Sibley now telling me all this? Besides poking all this fun at me, Mark knew it was too late for me to catch the last train back to Glacier Park. The only way I could try to catch Cosley again would have been to have hiked after him over Ahern pass. It would probably take me some time to get ready and the clock was running.

Let's face it. Things were stacked against me. First Cosley was well rested, and now he was provisioned. Second, he had a four or more hours head start on me. Third, Cosley was a stronger snowshoer and hiker (when he wasn't faking sickness or terminal death).

Joe Cosley faked being sick with me, and I'm a crusty ranger. He tried the same thing, and with his age he pleaded leniency from the court and the Commissioner fell for it. His friends certainly got Cosley out just as soon as possible. The timing seemed to be perfect.

* * * *

Logan Creek Ranger Station as it looked in 1997

Joe Cosley had many friends around the country, at Belton and others at Apgar. They must have been excited for Joe and to get back at the Park. Knowing Cosley a bit, he could have told them that if they helped him get away quickly, he would not disappoint any of them. The stories they could tell others for the rest of their days.

What still amazes me the most is that Cosley's fine was paid and he was released so quickly after the trial. It was like clock work. There was a plan and it was being carried out right on time.

Charlie drove Cosley 20 miles up along Lake McDonald past McDonald Falls and on up the valley past Avalanche Creek to the end of the road at Logan Creek where the patrol cabin is. There was no Logan Pass back then.

They would have said their good-byes as Howe drove and Cosley finished eating. At the trail head, with his pack on his back and the snowshoes in his hand, Cosley would have been off on the run. He knew the way home from here.

If Charlie drove the car at only 20 miles per hour it would have only taken one hour to get to the trailhead. I figure Cosley started his run about 2:00 that afternoon.

Cosley had a beaver cache hid somewhere in Belly River. Probably there were two locations. Waterton pelts in Canada and Belly River pelts in his cache near the boundary line or close to his camp where I arrested him.

Cosley didn't want to lose his cache of furs because beaver were paying from $25 for small to up to $50 a piece for good sized pelts that year. Cosley had about 55 beaver hides. I heard where Cosley sold them in Lethbridge or Medicine Hat.

*   *   *   *

The Judgment

I later learned that the Park Commissioner found Joseph Clarence Cosley guilty on all charges and fined him $25 for having firearms in the Park and $100.00 for having 7 traps, 3 muskrat hides and 1 beaver carcass in his possession. Cosley was sentenced to 90 days in jail. Joe pleaded guilty but did not accept responsibility. He said the traps were not his and the park could keep them. Cosley, in his soft spoken voice continued. He said he found the muskrat hides on a trail and the beaver parts were food. He said he actually thought he was camped in Canada. He asked for leniency as he was so sick, was dying of a terminal illness and would die in jail within days. His sickness and dying of a terminal illness were lies. There was no way this bird was going to die in jail. His sentence was shortened to 30 days and that was suspended because he was so ill, old and dying. I was upset. I was mad. I wasn't allowed to testify as to how Cosley faked, several times, being sick with me and with Tom Whitcraft.

Cosley's traps, the muskrat pelts, the .22 rifle, and beaver parts were confiscated[77] by the park and Cosley's fine of $125 stayed. He could be released on bail as soon as Cosley could raise 100 dollars.

So, that was the capture and release of Joe Cosley. Only a fine of a $100 for trapping and hunting in the park for 16 years after Glacier was made a National Park. And he got his 30 days in jail suspended. The park officials knew better than I that this old time trapper would have a beaver cache because he had been trapping this area for 20 years before it was made a park. That's a total of 36 years of trapping.

The park should have known. If Cosley's trapping brought him $5,000 each year for those 19 years Belly River was a park that would be close to $100,000 and he only got a fine of $100.

Cosley had been trapping all the way up from the Canadian side. All those beaver ponds from the Beebe Flat and above on the west (remember the old road that goes around, a lot of beaver in there) and the east side of the river and over in the Slide Lake area. He was also trapping all over in the Waterton Park area but that is a separate question with just Waterton.

The Backroom Boys

As soon as the westbound train had arrived in Belton, Cosley was taken to Park Headquarters. According to Bill Sibley, the Park wanted to talk to Cosley before the trial, and Cosley wanted to talk to them. We don't know what the Park leadership had to say to Cosley, but Sibley remarked that Cosley insisted on talking with Martin, his dad. Charlie Howe was also called for.

Cosley reassured the superintendent that he would not try to escape from them. He reminded that he came in peacefully and even helped carry some evidence in his backpack. Besides, he was too sick to go any where so why would he escape. He just wanted the trial to be over. When Martin Sibley arrived, both he and Cosley were allowed to visit, unsupervised, in the next room.

"Once they were alone," Bill told Dorothy Brading of Columbia Falls, "Cosley partially undid his sash and showed Martin a hand gun Cosley had under his waist band."

Cosley told Sibley that he could have shot the young kid, as he called Heimes, any time he wanted to. However, once he realized he was

---

77 Nobody seems to know where Cosley's .22 rifle, his traps, muskrat pelts and beaver parts are today.

going to be taken into Belton, he decided he would go peacefully and go and visit some of his good friends. And he had a plan that he had been working on for three days and nights and he needed their help.

Howe was also "allowed" to see Cosley and once again, in private. Howe was contacted by the Park and was invited to come and talk to Joe. When he arrived he, too, spoke with Joe alone unbothered in the room next to the office.

Having studied Joe Cosley for decades, this meeting in the back room so-to-speak, was a typical element in many of Cosley stories. All this is hearsay, but I think that its pretty much the way it happened. Other sources concur.

CHAPTER 18

THE RACE TO CACHE IN as told by Heimes

Get Ready. Set. Go!

I called Park Headquarters and told them what I had heard. They told me to get ready to leave in the morning to try to get to the furs. Getting ready was like living in the army (to hurry up and wait). There was no place for me to go so I had to wait.

I was already planning to return in the morning anyway. Around 5:00 PM the park called Clarence Willey at the Lake McDonald Ranger Station located at the head of McDonald and told him to try to catch Cosley. We knew Cosley's route and Willey was to catch him.

There was no storm on at the time and it was clear. Cosley's tracks[78] would have been easy to follow, but I don't think there was any man in the country who could catch Joe Cosley on snowshoes. While I was faster than he in short sprints, Cosley could continue at the run (on foot or on snowshoes) for hours. Cosley was the best man on snowshoes in the country. He could go a hundred miles in a day on snowshoes when he was younger. Cosley had snowshoed for most of his life, running traplines all winter long since he was a kid.

At a much earlier time I had heard that Cosley went on foot all the way, in one day, from the Polebridge Ranger Station northward up Bowman Creek and Lake over Brown Pass then eastward down Olson Creek past Lake Francis and Janet to Goat Haunt Ranger Station at the head of Waterton Lake, then north along the west side of the lake to the

[78] The surface of the snow at that altitude would freeze early in the evening, allowing Joe to walk on top without using his snowshoes. This would have enabled him to negotiate the treacherous Aherne Pass in the dark. Ernie Haug and DeLance Strate both told Frank Goble that Joe travelled all night.

Waterton town site, just to take in a dance. That would be over 35 miles one way. After the Waterton dance Cosley returned to Polebridge for work the next morning. That would have been a trip of 70 miles.

Clarence followed Cosley's tracks for ten miles to the snowline (6,000') just short of the Highline Trail. Clarence was a big husky fellow but was not a runner nor a real expert snowshoer and finally came back and phoned. He found Cosley's tracks but at Highline Trail. Said Cosley had too much of a head start and was getting further ahead all the time. Clarence could tell by Cosley's snowshoe tracks that his pace was at the run and so he gave it up. Willey hadn't taken his snowshoes and there was no way he could keep up, let alone try to overtake Cosley.

As I made preparations in West Glacier to return the next day it was obvious that Cosley had been planning this escape trek for days. He was well rested and now well provisioned. He had lied about his illness and his timing was perfect. I knew he was a liar, but the park had bought his whole illness and dying thing. So after several days I was exhausted and Cosley was rested and probably 30 miles from here going down to Helen Lake at the trot. (20 miles to Logan Creek Patrol Cabin and 10 miles of his 30 miles to his camp).

I couldn't get started until the next day because I had to go back by train to East Glacier. The last passenger train for that day had already left, and the next one going east was the next morning.

The park called me up in Belton and updated me on Clarence Willey and what he found. All night long I kept thinking about what Cosley would be doing and where he was. I could not sleep. Cosley was on his way back into Belly River.

Coslcy had obviously planned this exit for the last couple of days. His plan probably started when Tom Whitcraft and Bert Barnes met me in the trees, and Cosley in desperation decided to come out peaceably. Every waking hour since then he was just adding details to the plan. I could see it all now. When Cosley reached snow level he would have put the snowshoes on and still keep right on running.

Cosley would have gone over Ahern Pass that afternoon. He started from where Charlie Howe dropped him off at about 2:00 in the afternoon. Cosley probably made it to Elizabeth before it was dark. Cosley was no doubt sober in more ways than one crossing Ahern Pass.

The park had *not* maintained Ahern Pass for years and Ahern has not been used since. But Cosley had helped build the Ahern Pass Trail and he knew the country so well that he could travel it even in the dark. Most of the high country in those mountains was snow covered and it is easy to see snow at night even with only a little moon.

Traveling on snowshoes in snow packed mountain means you don't even need to follow the trail. You can just cut through and beeline it straight to the destination.

Joe Cosley on snowshoes. Notice his long legs the packsack on his back.
Photo courtesy of Richard West

Half a mile north of the falls he could have crossed the Belly River and cut through the clearing in front of the Ranger Station, then crossed the Belly River back over to the west side again. Or he could have stayed on the west side of the river all the way to his camp. His final cut through would have been from the straight stretch of the Belly River about ¾ of a mile upstream from Three Mile. He would have headed straight north directly to his camp.

At first light Cosley would be up and going at full speed. Sunrise (Mountain Standard Time) in these foothills for May 11 was at 6:03 a.m. with first light 46 minutes before that. He would have had plenty of time to round up his trap sets, harvesting any additional beaver and mink caught and take them with his cache of furs into Canada. His camp was only a mile and a half from the Canadian border.

Cosley could have been out of Belly River with all of his cache by early morning with time to spare. Once in Canada, he would have plenty of time to prepare the recent pelts harvested. He would be laughing because he would be laughing at me *and* the Park.

Let's face it. Cosley could have taken his cache of furs into Canada long before I even got to bed Friday night let alone got on the train at Belton to return to East Glacier.

Even if Cosley needed to make two trips to haul all his stuff out of Belly River and into Canada, he still would have been out of Glacier by early morning. I wish I had a picture of Cosley's grin when he crossed into Canada with all his cache and gear.

However, Cosley traveled it, he made it through. I think he made it in record time. This was not a two-person race.

As Paul Harvey says, "Here is the rest of the story"... Lloyd Sanders claims that his Dad Duke Sanders and another friend had gotten word of Joe's trouble and moved in quick to help. They rescued Cosley's fur, traps and supplies. This information comes from an interview Edwin Knox did with Lloyd Sanders.

Trapper Joe Cosley and Cosley Marked Tree
Photos courtesy of Julia Nelson

Time, Distance, Arrival at Cosley Camp with cut throughs
(less 2 miles saved with cut throughs to his camp)

Total Distance	Average Speed (mph)	Hours Taken	Trailhead Time	ETA
26.5 miles	7	3:47	2:00 pm	6:17 pm
26.5 miles	6	4:25	2:00 pm	6:55 pm
26.5 miles	5	5:18	2:00 pm	7:48 pm

CHAPTER 19

CATCH COSLEY'S CACHE, as told by Heimes

SATURDAY, MAY 11
Weather stormy

The more I thought about Cosley's race to get his furs, the more discouraged I was at the outcome.

Then I thought the Park should have sent Lou Hanson to get to Cosley's Secret Camp on Friday afternoon. Hanson could have driven to Canada via Coutts / Sweetgrass before they closed, and by driving all night he could have been at Cosley's Camp long before midnight.

One problem. Hanson didn't know where the camp was. Tom knew approximately where it was, and I knew exactly where it was. Of course, Tom and I were still in Belton until Saturday morning.

All "Should Haves" Come Too Late

After a sleepless night thinking about what tomorrow would bring, worried about my dogs at the Ranger Station, and still mad at the Park for letting Cosley off so easy and so soon, I was ready to leave Belton hours before the 11:05 a.m. train arrived.

The Park met me to see me off and filled me in. Lou Hanson was to meet me and Tom at the train station, drive us to Canada, and walk with me to Cosley's camp. I wasn't going to walk.

I told the park what I thought of the way they let Cosley go. I didn't hold anything back, and that was the end of me for a number of years.

To make my day, the train was late. I remembered that the same train was also late 3½ years ago when I was transferred to Belly River with my trunk and supplies for the station. What a slow train ride that was. It seemed even slower than it was arriving here Thursday.

I counted the minutes always looking at my watch. The station master seems to be the only person working for the Great Northern Railway that was concerned about keeping a schedule. The train engineer never kept to a schedule it seemed to me.

Of course I kept thinking of where Cosley would be now.

Arrived at East Glacier at 1:12 and late. There the assistant chief ranger Lou Hanson, who used to be stationed at Goat Haunt on Waterton, picked us up. He had my two pair of snowshoes in the back. We drove 90 miles to Babb, on into Alberta through Cardston, to Mountain View, then further west to J. J. West's Ranch. This was the first time we didn't have to have an RCMP escort.

We talked on the way. He, too, was upset about the light sentence and the early release. Because of that, here we were racing to get back to Cosley's camp. Time was against us because of Cosley's head start and having to wait for the train that morning. Now it was raining.

However, Hanson disagreed with me that Cosley could have hiked all the way to Canada at his advanced age and being sick. Tom agreed with Lou, and the two of them talked most of the way to Mountain View. I just ran over the figures in my mind to the contrary.

We drove near the first ford on the Belly River in Canada and left the vehicle there. J.J. West's ranch is on the east side of the Belly River and Cosley's camp was on the other.

We traveled the rest of the way by horse. I left my two pair of snowshoes at the ranch. It was the 11th of May. It took four days to get Cosley into Headquarters and the next day for trial and the following day for us to get back.

Tom went as far as the Canadian Belly River Station and returned to his station. Lou Hanson went back in with me intending to take out Cosley's camp and equipment etc. By the time Lou Hanson and I got to Cosley's camp, the camp was all gone. It wasn't much of a camp. There was a pole on an angle that Cosley had draped a white canvas tarp over to shelter his sleeping area. On the ground under the pole was a bunch of pine bows held together by poles on both sides. Cosley had a few blankets on top of the bows. His fire pit was to the south of the lean-to. That had been his camp.

Everything was gone. All tracks had been completely erased. Everything had just disappeared except for the pole and some beaver parts and an otter spreader. But what bothered me the most was that when I captured and arrested Cosley I didn't have a chance to look for the beaver hides and other furs. Now Cosley had beat me to them. The park gave him a $100 fine and a suspended jail sentence. They should have given him the full 30 days in jail or at least five or ten days to give me the chance to find his cache of furs.

Cosley's former camp used for trapping in Belly River District, Glacier National Park. Taken May 12, 1929 Picture courtesy of Joe Heimes taken by Lou Hanson

Return To The Ranger Station

Lou stayed with me at the Belly River Ranger Station. I was tired and wanted to check on my dogs and horses.

As I arrived I could tell the dogs were hungry. They could hear me coming and I hollered out. I fed my dogs as fast as I could. They were glad to see me and they were starved. They had not been fed in days.

Usually if you went to headquarters you would be gone a week and if you didn't have some one come up there and feed your dogs they would die. I had made a deal with Bert Barnes, Canadian Ranger in Waterton, for him to go up and feed my dogs. He knew I was going to be gone most of a week. I believe that Barnes fed my dogs twice but he should have gone again. The dogs went hungry for two days. That really upset me.

The next day Lou was heading home and I rode with him to see Cosley's camp again. The weather was now sunny and Lou wanted to take another picture in case the other did not turn out. Tom Whitcraft came but didn't stay.

I continued to patrol my district for several days to find trapper signs but no other sign. On May 19 I blew the beaver dam. I put in four shots. The next day I rode to the West's and told him the road was clear and to get my mail.

When J. J. West brought in our supply wagon he also brought my two pair of snowshoes.

I decided to sell my dog team and sleigh. Bert Barnes said he wanted to buy my dog team and sleigh, but I would never inflict Barnes on my dogs again.

I arranged to take my dogs and sleigh back to Rivieres for $100.00.

I soon had my vegetable garden all planted. There were supplies that I did not receive with my recent wagon load, and so I left to go to Cardston to get some things.

More Of The Story

A month later I received a report from J. Ross Eakin, Glacier Park Superintendent. He said that he sent the following description in his monthly report to Washington D. C.

> *On May 6th Ranger Joe Heimes of the Belly River District apprehended Joe Cosley, a famous Indian trapper, subdued him after a terrific struggle, and brought the prisoner to Belton on May 9th. The U.S. Commissioner fined him $125. The Indian is over 6 feet and weighs 180 lbs. Joe is five feet six inches and weighs 145 lbs. The story is now being written for a magazine and will be one of the epics of the National Parks.*

Well, everything Superintendent Eakin wrote was true, but it didn't tell the whole story.

Other stories the Park heard was that Cosley was operating a game ranch for anyone that wanted game.[79] If a person wanted an elk to eat, Joe Cosley would bring them one. Cosley had lots of friends on both sides of the boundary.

"These are not things a Ranger in a National Park should be doing," concludes Joe Heimes.

Rest Of The Story

While researching for this book I learned there was more to this story. Some friends of Joe Cosley would regularly visit Cosley at his trapping camp in Glacier and take him food. After Cosley had been arrested, Duke Sanders saw all the tracks and knew there was something amiss with the camp. There were no beaver parts on the pole over the fire and the fire was cold — a telltale sign that something was terribly

---

[79] DeLance Strate told Goble they always hunted there while Joe was the Ranger.

wrong. And so even before Cosley went to trial, Duke Sander picked up everything at Cosley's camp and took it to the Sander Ranch in Alberta.

Cosley would have seen how clean his camp was, and that was a sign to him that Duke had been there. He would have gone directly to Duke's that night, and probably had supper with them and slept in a warm bed. Then the two of them would have hauled out every trap and hide harvested in the early morning. This was the same Duke Sanders that took Joe Heimes' things into the Belly River Station when Heimes was first assigned to Belly River 3 ½ years before.

There was more to Cosley's reception and homecoming in Canada. Bud Spencer from Lethbridge told me that once Joe Cosley made it back to his camp, he got everything out including his cache of furs. Then a friend of Cosley's, DeLance Strate, drove Cosley to Waterton so that Cosley could buy Waddy Foster's boat. Then Cosley loaded his furs and traps and rowed down to Winnipeg[80] and sold the furs and the boat for a great price. Cosley then moved up North, first in northern Saskatchewan.

What was in Cosley's Cache?

D. Strate and E. Haug told Frank Goble that Cosley's cache on the U.S. side contained 73 beaver.

The Boat Was A Canoe

Walter (Waddy) B. Foster worked summers for Waterton Lakes National Park until at least 1956. He lived in Waterton and "was responsible for much of the stone and log work on many of the early government buildings and private dwellings within the townsite," says Rob Watt Senior Park Warden.

From his home just west of Creston, Waddy Foster told me this:

"It was just after supper the second Sunday in May, 1929 when there was a knock at my door (in Waterton). I answered the door to find Joe Cosley in a hurry. Joe wanted to buy my canvas covered canoe, that was painted red, to take his cache of furs down river to Medicine Hat, Alberta, from there to catch the train east to market his winters harvest at higher prices.

"I had a hard time getting Joe to come into the house. He was really in a hurry and wanted to just purchase the canoe and go. But I wanted to talk, and so I welcomed my friend to come in for a visit. He finally did come inside and had some pie at my insistence.

[80] Frank Goble states that Cosley had plenty of money on this occasion, he had just sold his 'reclaimed' furs in Pincher Creek.

"I still insisted he take my 17' canoe and it was free[81] to Joe and that was that. Joe bargained with me to go and get the diamond ring out of the Aspen tree near Belly River just south of the line at Beebe Flats in exchange for the canoe. I knew of the stories of Cosley's romance and refusal by the young lady in Mountain View, and I had heard that Joe hid the diamond ring in a tree.

"This night Joe told me exactly where the tree was located and which tree it was buried in and how far up from the ground to find it.

"Just to strike a deal, I agreed to the exchange. But out of respect for Joe's love for this woman, I never did go and get the diamond ring. I never intended to.

"Before leaving, Joe told me he had never told anybody else about where the diamond was actually located," stated Foster.

I asked him if he never intended to go and get "Joe's ring" because there was no ring in the first place? He smiled and said, "Yes." When further questioned he told me that he knew Cosley for what he was, a poor trapper who when he got some good money he seemed to blow the whole thing in weeks and would be broke again. It was always "next year country" or "next furbearer harvest" with Joe Cosley.

He said, "I have heard that lots of other people had been told by Cosley to go up and get his diamond ring, and many went up there. They didn't find a ring. If there really was a ring worth something, then Joe himself would have gone up there and retrieved it because he was always broke. Then there was the flood of 1923. If there really was a ring then surely the flood of '23 would have washed it down stream because it washed that side of the bank away."

---

[81] Goble saw Waddy Foster's canoe many times and it was red. He adds that Waddy like to embellish his stories. E. Haug and D. Strate both told Goble that Joe paid $5.00 for the canoe.

CHAPTER 20

CROWING IN CARDSTON[82]

Joe Heimes had been looking for the day that he could travel to Cardston and this was to be the morning. Here's Heimes in Cardston.

Belly River Ranger Station, Heimes continues telling his account: June 8, 1929. Weather clear and warm.

As soon as I arrived in Cardston to get supplies for the Ranger Station I learned that Joe Cosley was telling stories all over Cardston about his escape from jail in Belton and how he out-raced the rangers to the cache of furs and won the race. It all sounded exciting, but there was no jail in Belton and he did not escape.

Some accounts painted me as a bad person for arresting Cosley in the first place. One person I talked to must have been a close friend with Cosley because he told me I was wrong to have arrested Cosley half a mile north of J. J. West's (about 2 miles north of the boundary in Canada) and that it was illegal for a U. S. Ranger to come into Canada to make an arrest.

---

[82] Cardston, Alberta is located at 49° 12'N, 113° 18'W. Named for Charles Ora Card (1839-1906), son-in-law of Brigham Young, who came to the present site of Cardston, on Lees Creek in 1886 from Utah, to establish new home for members of the Church of Jesus Christ of Latter-day Saints. "Ton" in Old English means "town." The following year, the main colony, consisting of ten families, arrived and took up squatter's rights since the official Dominion Land Survey had not yet been completed. A crude survey was done by Mormons, and J. S. Dennis, D. L. S., re-surveyed the land in the fall of 1887. Cardston was granted a post office in 1892, became a village in 1898 and a town in 1901. Ora Card was the town's first mayor.

Where do these people get their information from. It sounded like another Joe Cosley story to me, you see. When I asked people where they had heard the account they were telling me, they said they read it in the newspaper.

There were accounts that I punished Cosley severely, taking him in to trial by dragging him behind my horse across the line and all the way to trial. They said I whipped Cosley with a bull whip and stabbed him repeatedly with my bowie knife. I was a bad person to them. I just smiled and went about my business. I have never seen a bowie knife or a bull whip except in the movies.

I met Cosley the last part of this trip in Cardston. The first time I met Cosley after the trial was in the Cahoon Hotel restaurant on main street. When I entered the door he saw me right away. He was about half through eating his meal. He got up and left his meal half eaten and walked out and never said a word to me or anyone.

I said to Cosley, "Where is my gold watch?" I didn't really want his gold watch,[83] and I didn't believe he even had one but I did stand up to him. As he walked by me I asked him, "What are all these stories I have been hearing about your escape and me treating you badly?" Cosley said nothing and just left in a hurry. "What lies have you been telling?"

He did not reply and he did not look me in the eye. He just looked straight ahead. He was out the door heading south down main street.

Cosley could not stand up to truth," said Heimes.

Tally The Take

Heimes found out that Cosley had sold 55 beaver,[84] 21 marten, and 22 mink hides in Lethbridge for a great price. I heard that Cosley had made a boat, like a row boat, and loaded his furs and went down the Belly River to Lethbridge. I had heard that Cosley, at times, sold his furs in Cardston at the Purina feed store, but not this year.

If Cosley had promised to repay his two friends in the West Glacier and Apgar who paid $50 dollars each, then Joe certainly had the money now. The price I heard, from the Robinhood flour man, that Cosley received for his poached, furs well over $4129 Canadian. That was a great price for a winter's work in those days.

Where are all the facts. I still don't know and perhaps never will. How do all these stories get started and be so divergent?

---

[83] Others have said Cosley did have an expensive pocket watch and it was silver.

[84] Cosley had in his beaver cache in Glacier 73 beaver, D. Strate and E. Haug, Cosley's long-time friends in Waterton; told Frank Goble.

The Cardston News

Fred Burton, the publisher and editor of the Cardston News told the author the following about Cosley's escape from Montana and the race to Canada.

Fred said that Cosley came in to see him in a terrible way. Cosley was not well; he was sick and dying. Cosley told of a crazy ranger south of the border, with the help of three others, had beat Cosley up near J. J. West ranch. Then they roped Cosley and dragged him all the way to Belton behind one of the horses. The whole story sounded strange to Fred.

Fred told Cosley he did not want to print that story because there was no proof — just Joe's side of the story. Fred also said that he didn't have the time to phone over to Belton to get their side of the story.

However, Cosley said some things that were probably true or at least they sounded true. Cosley also begged Fred as old war buddies to print the story. Fred asked Cosley when were they ever buddies but Cosley was determined to tell the story before he died.

Fred agreed to print part of the story, but that it would be "by the book" with direct quotes from Cosley telling his side of the story and lots of language that this story had not been confirmed and the public had better consider its source. And the story ran near the back of the paper under some ads.

"Well," remembered Fred, "the story got around town like a forest fire. It seemed to be the talk of the town in Cardston and all the way to Lethbridge. The Lethbridge paper picked it up as did Calgary."

Fred was shocked to see Cosley at the grocery store a few days later and Joe was not dying or as ill as he was before. Fred knew he had been tricked by Cosley: lied to was the better description.

Fred felt bad about the story based on knowing Cosley and past stories. The next issue, Fred printed a follow-up story to set the record straight. He had called to get the US side of the story and there was a large difference between what was being said on the streets of Cardston and reality.

"The trouble was," stated Burton, "Cosley was going around and talking to people all over town. He met them on main street and in the public places and he told them his full story." "He used the little bit that was printed in the paper as proof that there was a story and that Joe was telling them more truth," remorsed Burton. Fred wouldn't print any more "experiences" of Joe Cosley ever again, and he told Cosley to get out of town and not come back.

Heimes' Last Meeting of Cosley

I needed more supplies in Cardston for the Ranger Station. I noticed a difference this trip from all my other trips to Cardston. Some people seemed reluctant to talk with me. However, others did talk to me and told me of Joe Cosley and more of his stories. Many of the stories were about the same as I had heard last trip but some other accounts sounded even further from the truth.

The next time I ran into Cosley was in the Cardston barbershop on Main Street a month later. He was sitting in the barber's chair. The barber was not busy, and when I walked in, they were just chewing the fat.

I went in to get a haircut. Haircuts in those days were just 50 cents. There was a bell that rang as the door was opened or closed. When I entered the door, Cosley looked and saw me and he just gets up and walks out. He would not even look at me when I talked to him. He just darted for the door.

"You liar!" I said. "What are all these lies you are telling all over town?" "Have you been poaching more beaver in Glacier Park?" That was all I was able to get in before the door closed and the bell jingled.

That barber was not very friendly toward me so maybe he was a friend of Cosley's. I went in for a haircut and not to chitchat.

"That's the last I saw him. Cosley just left and had nothing to say and was in a real hurry to get away from me," stated Joe Heimes.

Fred Burton told the author that Cosley returned the following year.

Cosley had the "gumption" to come into the paper and want another story printed. "I threw a block at him but Cosley ducked and then left. I never saw Cosley again."

"The next I heard of Cosley he was up in Northern Saskatchewan north of Prince Albert trapping up there until his death," ended Burton.

Even to this day, there are many who have heard Cosley Stories and are more than pleased he got away with beating the US officials to the cache of illegal furs. They are excited.

The problem still exists that people on both sides of the border just do not know the whole story to base their judgment on. The Cosley version of bias continues to mislead Canadians and Americans. Cosley's much truth but some lies continues to cause people to root for Cosley, the little guy, compared to the big corporation.

The Cosley version has a ring of David versus Goliath. Most people root for David, and they are glad that Cosley won the race. They rejoice that Cosley had the last laugh at Glacier Park. For some, it is even a case of Canada vs. the United States, and Canada won.

CHAPTER 21

THE MAJOR MOVE NORTH

Bud Spencer's Last Meeting With Cosley

"Bud" Spencer states that he met his friend Joe the summer of 1930 in Cardston. Cosley had been up north for the previous trapping season.

Spencer met Cosley at the Cahoon Hotel, and they visited long after they finished eating. Cosley told how he needed solitude and the only place he could find that was deep in the woods of Northern Alberta. Cosley said he also wanted to be alone and needed to be as far away from civilization as he could get. The north was the least populated.

Bud continues.

"Cosley told me that he was just in Cardston for a few days to pick up his traps and other gear from friends, and then head north to get his trapline in shape for the coming season. He said the fur was better up north and that he had built a fine cabin where nobody could find him." Luck was beginning to change for Joe Cosley but he would not admit to it for a few years more.

Cosley had a cash project he wanted to complete before he went up north. He was doubly paid for this adventure. He originally sold this expedition to the Alberta Government to survey the rivers flowing through Medicine Hat. Secondly, Joe resold it to the Albertan; who ran the story September 12, 1929, under the headline:

Exploring Alberta In A Canoe

The Account of a One-Man Expedition Into Some of the Odd Corners of our Province

By Joseph C. Cosley, Cardston

This is simply the narrative of an expedition carried out by the writer of the South Saskatchewan River in the interests of the Natural Resources Intelligence Service. It may be found interesting as demonstrating that in spite of the advance of civilization, the day of Western adventure is not yet by any means over.

During eight days on the Waterton River, before the high water, I had much difficulty in going over many shallow rapids and sand bars. But when the Belly River was reached, the high water from the Old Man and St. Mary's Rivers overtook me, and I had trouble in handling my canoe owing to the swift flow and undercurrent of that great river. In the meantime a cloudburst occurred in the mountains; especially at the head waters of the Bow River it caused havoc to the timber along the streams and shore-lines the whole length of the upper waters. At the mouth of the Bow River the surging waters of that cloudburst had also arrived. The terror of the foaming, muddy swirl, backs high, rushing out of the confluence into the South Saskatchewan, was like the pent-up force boiled over in torrents. Logs and broken timber and whole lengths of trees, snags and large roots, lumber from tumble-down houses, raced down the river at high speed. The limbs and long roots, like flexible tentacles of some gigantic beast, struck with tremendous impact like living arms. The whole mass was tossed about like match wood. Islands of undermined banks with scrubby trees swaying to and fro floated swiftly by intermittently as other material things churned in the swirling terror at the rear. Large trees, at intervals, struck bottom forcibly, and the hind ends rose upwards and flopped forward with a loud splash, causing tremendous waves which broke against the shores like a mighty tidal wave. The Belly River, which now formed the Saskatchewan, poured forth its water with violence through high banks.

For a week the high water continued, and I was obliged to seek safety on an island with water flowing throught the trees all around. During this overflowing torrent, I saw drowned horses, cattle, sheep and some chickens drift in the debris. On this occasion I saw two dead beavers. The only account I can give for their destruction is that they met their death in the dens under the banks which caved in upon them and later washed out and exposed them there.

An accident happened to me during this great flood, and I was mauled seriously by the swell which threatened at frequent intervals to capsize my canoe. One June 22 I reached Medicine Hat, not any too sure of my footing.

Owen McClung tells of when Joe Cosley bought five 12" boards (3/4" thick) to make a boat. He bought the boards from Bud Beck at the lumber yard in Cardston. Cosley built my design of three boards on the floor and one on each side. For the front he had a 4" x 4" and a plank for the transom in the back.

And he took it down to Lees Creek and filled it with rocks to sink. That tightened it up. Cosley told the lumber yard that from Cardston he was going to the Flin Flon in it.

> I proceeded again this fall in view of completing this trip to Empress. I made a boat at Cardston and launched it in St. Mary's River, two miles from the town. But there was not enough water to float my boat over the numerous rapids and waterfalls which I came upon at short intervals. There was a canyon for ten miles, and in that "hell's own time" was encountered. I must have waded two-thirds of the river tugging, pushing and hauling the boat over boulders and sand bars to get to the confluence of the river, almost a hundred miles away.

So it was. Joe's article ran for another 16 column inches and ended with discovery of gas bubbles rising from the river downstream from the Hat. He lit a match to the gas which produced a blue flame, natural gas in the wilds.

Cosley wrote lots of letters to friends. A year earlier while he was in Columbia Falls for the summer he wrote to Mrs. Maggie Ivins on July 17th, 1928.

> Dear Friend:-
>
> I am writing to you this evening, knowing that you would like to hear from an old trapper and friend who has roamed the mountains and valleys of the west. And his diamond ring is hidden in Belly River country and you are welcome to get it if you can find it.
>
> I am resting peacefully and thinking pleasant things all alone as usual, for I am a lonely man, so said Carline Lockhart once in her history of Mankind. I am writing some stories, I guess you will know why I am alone, ah ah.

This was one of many Joe Cosley sent to her. He also sent letters to several other people. Like most people growing older, he reflected back on the good old times shared together with friends.

I would like to include some parts of these letters to share with you the flair he had for trapping, even when things were not going great. With Cosley's move to the North, he was no longer just 20 or 40 miles away from his friends, he was 400 or 800 miles away. It was not that easy to return for a visit anymore.

Mrs. Margaret Ivens — Edmonton, Alta.
Cardston, Alta. — Jun. 26th, 1932
Dear Friend:-

I would have liked to make a trip as far as Cardston and see my old friends and especially the "Rich Widow" who is looking for me all the time and me always thinking of her, ah ah. This sound like a dream, but it is not, it is the real thing, for I have always loved the "Rich Widow" in my mind and never told her so and it might be a thing of the past now in the imagination of the widow If she had known a few years ago. But it is not, it is still glowing hot.

Ah, those good old days that's gone forever. However, if I do well next spring I will come down from above and see what I can do for her lovely neck.

We all had very hard winter; I am having bad luck, seem that I can never get out of it. Perhaps some day I will see better time. Yours as ever -- friend Jos.

Mrs. Margaret Ivens, — Edmonton, Alberta
Beazer, Alberta. — Sept. 11th, 1932.
Dear Friend:-

I am leaving here on Tuesday the 13th for my trapping grounds in the north to be there until June the 10th next year. I will write you a letter or two during the winter and tell you how I am faring with my traps. Perhaps next year I will be able to pay you a visit as I expect to do a little better this time.

Got a letter from Ernie Haug of Waterton Lakes who said all is well with him and wife. He told me many things concerning the people of that district.

If things are good in the Great Bear Lake District in the spring, I am going up there early and see if I could locate some rich claims for myself and I will write to you always.

Yours as ever, Jos.

Mrs. Margaret Ivens | Fort McMurray Postoffice
Beezer, Alberta. | Feb. 14th, 1933.

Dear Maggie:-

Ten men on showshoes and teams of dogs and tobbogans on their way to Great Bear Lake bought down your letter and I surely was well pleased to read it with the news of Cardston and vicinities. I also got one from Margaret West who was just detained with writing this letter when she should be going to a big supper preparatory to her trip to Salt Lake City, in the morrow.

That fox I was going to send you they say it is a Samson Fox, a woolly cross, as if the long hair had been plucked and the fur only remained. It is not tanned and would cost you something to have it tanned and made. However, I shall send it to you if you want it. I am well and eating plenty of moose meat. The hide of a moose is like a cow, is no good. How are things around Mountain View.

Your friend the trapper.

Mrs. Maggie Ivens | Edmonton, Alberta
Beazer, Alta. | August 16th, 1933

Dear Friend:-

I know I will not starve while out here, I am a good trapper and hunter, ah ah. I have a net and when I feel like eating fish I can set the net. There is a lot of whitefish in the river and if I care to catch whitefish I can set my net at once when I get there and catch a whole barrel and smoke them for the winter. There is plenty of rabbits and chickens around my cabins to keep me alive.

Very good wishes to you and all, I am, Yours very truly, Jos.

Mrs. Margaret Ivens | Fort McMurray, Alta.
Beezer, Alta. | March 2nd, 1934

I left in Sept. for my trapping ground to get away from the hard times in Edmonton. I got a good supply of provisions to do me all winter and I feel satisfied of what I did as the winter was indeed severe here, ranging from 50° to 68° below zero. It was so cold that I was not able to go out during these cold spells. Saw several birds and some rabbits had parished in the cold and found one with frozen feet.

Saw a squaw going to Fort McMurray with her toboggan and six dogs and was covered with bear-skin fur and fox parkay and legging made out of buckskin will headed and heavy mittens that reach up to her elbows. Her face was literally covered with fur of ermines and a long black robe-like muffler of wolverine fur intertwined her robust neck. She was smoking clay-pipe of tobacco mixed with kinnicinnick. I happened to be on the river shivering from the cold and the squaw was walking behind her toboggan to limber up her legs, I guessed. A papoose was muffled up in the toboggan and was crooning happily.

When I got home I perceived I had two fingers slightly froze and my cheeks crusted with frost-bite. God deliver the old squaw, she got home safe alright.

I caught several red foxes, some crosses and one silver-grey last fall, did not trap during the winter, everything had left the country. I am going to do some spring trapping down to the delta, a hundred miles down the river where rats are plentiful they say. I saw several Indians with squaws already have gone down with their dogs and sleighs. Beautiful days here now, looks like spring and the chichadees are singing "Spring Soon" on the trees around about.

Mrs. Margaret Ivens
Beazer, Alberta,

Fort McMurray, Alta.
Sept. 1st, 1934

Dear Margaret:-

I have arrived here at my cabin about two weeks ago, being so tired of city life and hearing so much of foreign language that I hasten to leave Edmonton where familiar sounds would please me more than Bohunk tongue.

I am fairly well and not too contented of being here all alone. There is nothing to be done yet and I am just staying in camp and reading a little. Have no ambition or no effort of stimulating the action of the mind to write a story like I used to have when I did a lot of writing. My mind is vacant, nothing in it and I am ashame to even write this uninterested letter lest you would say to wake up and sir your cobweb mind.

I have my cabin located one mile in the woods from the Athabaska to avoid visitors coming here. A visitor in the shape of a bear came and annoy me the other day and I shot at him several times but no damage was done as my rifle was only a .22.

I bought some coal oil and a lamp to use this winter instead of a lot of candles which cost money. I have all my supplies for the winter at camp and when it turns colder I will go out and kill a moose or deer. There is two months yet before I can trap, we usually begin in Nov. The beauty of it is, is that I have all my winter's wood cut and are piled up near the cabin, have chopped the fire-wood last spring and it is dried now. This is all I can say to you, with best of wishes to you as I close my letter, I am as ever, yours very truly, Jos.

Mrs. Margaret Ivens
Beazer, Alta, Can.

Cabin On-The-Athabaska
Fort McMurray, Alta.
January 28th, 1935.

My Dear Very Rich-Widow:-

"I had some bad luck last fall just before the snow fell. My cabin No. 2 was destroyed by fire when I was away, burned up a large wolf-skin, a fox fur and everything else that was in. Beside another thing linked itself with this bad luck was that I capsize in the river and drown my rifle. Although I bought a new rifle things went wrong which made me lost the best part of my trapping season. I rebuilt a new cabin about the time when the cold weather was setting in and I couldn't endure the cold that those frozen green logs produced inside by severe cold without inspite of a small wood-stove burning steadily all night. The nights are very long too, fifteen and sixteen hours of blackness raging with intense zero-temperatures and continue almost the same all through the day. When spring fetches wormer days I will go and finish the cabin suitable for next fall and by that time the logs will have dried to keep inside with greater heat. Now, I am living in my cabin No. 1, near the river, have nothing to do, there is nothing stirring, too cold for any animal of the fur-bearing kinds and even for man to venture out in such temperatures. I killed a deer and with its meat and other things to live on I do not need to go out in the cold. There are lots who are worse than I an, these poor Indians and lazy whiteskins are starving, some of them, too lazy to go and kill a moose. This should have been looked after before the cold had set in and provided themselves with lots of meat. I have plenty of potatoes, carrots, parsnips, and cabbage in my seller and plenty of lard, sugar and all kinds of things to last me all winter until June, beside I have money in my pockets.

You asked me to write you a letter and as I have lots of time in doing so I am writing this one for you. There is a family of Bohemian, a man and his wife are living ten miles from me and they invited me for Christmas. She made me a present of a pair of mittens of her own make, she cooked a nice dinner -- a big turkey. I have finished u a new book with pictures in it like the other book. I want you to see it and have Babe read it for you. Write me again -- Jos

Mrs. Maggie Ivens, Fort McMurray, Alta.
Cardston, Alta. Feb. 10th, 1937
Dear Friend:-

I am still trapping and occupying the same cabin in the north. I have had a little hard luck by cutting a big gash on my foot last fall, although it healed well, I fear my long hiking shall be curtailed. I have not made anything this season due to the scarcity of furs and the food which is also scarce have driven them to other country. But even of my condition, I will come back to Edmonton and spend two or three months next summer. Perhaps I might see you at the Fair about July. You scarcely know how fast us older folks are growing old these days and one by one will be led to the grave before we know it. However, I am in constant thought of my old friends whom I had the good fortune to associate in intertainments and in dances. Now the time I met you at the old minister church at Mountain View when Bessie Coldwell and Dug. Oland presided over music.

I hope the Rich Widow may never grow old and that some day we may find ourselves standing on the dock of one old steamboat landing place, up there at Waterton Lakes. Perhaps we might go on that trip we had proposed many years ago and see the old trap-lines I had made in the early 90's and those of Kootenai Brown's.

as ever-friend Jos.

Mrs. Maggie Ivens | Edmonton, Alberta
North Lethbridge, Alta | July 13th, 1940

My Dear Rich Widow:-

I am still doing some trapping in the far north and doing well with my traps. But do better with my pen and MSS.

I have returned about a week ago with load of furs, waiting for auction which will take place about Aug. 8th. I am feeling good and feel I am young again.

very truly yours, Jos.

Mrs. Maggie Ivens | Edmonton, Alberta
North Lethbridge | February 4th, 1943

Dear Friend:-

I am writing other stories for pass time, no one to bother me in my room, no body come and is just as well because I do not care for company.

Everything lovely here after the big storm. The people seemed scared of that big snow storm, but I didn't, rather enjoyed it, for I am use to bad weathers in the north. Snow is clean and white and refreshing. A snow-bath usually is good for the body, makes one smart and lively. Indians have been known to take such baths and so is the white man in the north, that's why those Indians live ever so long, for it makes them healthy.

This winter I have contracted bad cold once or twice and felt bad for a while. If I had been in the woods in the north, no such thing would happen to me.

am sending lots of good wishes--Jos.

This is the last letter we, the public, have of Cosley that he sent to Ivins. In the fall he would return to his trapline and cabin for his last time.

"In a hand written will Joe Cosley left his few belongings and his trapline to Dee Strate, the oldest son of Cosley's good friend DeLance Strate. Dee was in the army at the time, stationed in Calgary." Frank Goble said that this statement was told to him by both DeLance and Dee Strate.

* * * *

The Way He Wanted It

As we near the end of this book, I would like to quote from Julia Nelson's excellent article that was published in the Canadian Cattlemen Magazine. There is no finer tribute to Julia and her writing than to quote from her story "JOE COSLEY – Trapper and Guide Extraordinary"

Julia Nelson writes:[85]

"After an eight-day search through the northern wilds of Saskatchewan, Constable J. McLeod and his Indian guide entered a trapper's log cabin 400 miles north of Prince Albert. This was on October 12, 1944. They found that Joe Clarence Cosley had dramatized his own miserable death as fully and effectively as he had his 74 years of vibrant, enthusiastic living."

"The last of his hundreds of stories had plot, suspense, and a gripping climax. In the diary lying near his bones he had not written: 'I am dying of scurvy,' He told instead of a sinister curse, creeping and deadly, visited by some unknown power upon this lonely house. The trapper before him had died here, from the curse, of course, and daily Joe outlined his own suffering:

'I am steadily growing weaker . . . I can hardly write . . . I have reached the end . . .' He was conscious to the last, of the interesting pathos of the situation."

"Too tired for the trip from Edmonton to Isle La Crosse, he hired a plane, the last few seasons, to take him and his equipment to his trapping grounds."

"It must have never occurred to him that he was old. He did get to the point, though, of thinking there might be a circumstance up there that he wouldn't be able to handle alone, for at 73, when he set out on what was to be his last trip, he said what he'd never said before:

'If I'm not back in May, send someone to look for me.'

"It wasn't a sad and regrettable ending. Anyone who ever knew Joe would tell you he wanted it that way," concludes Julia Nelson.

* * * *

Joe had the ability to slip in or out of people's lives without being detected. In his youth, Joe was known as Sahgahnuhquudoo "Cloud Appearing". Joe Cosley was a man of mystery and that was the way he wanted its.

He remains the greatest mountain man in these parts. He will always be Belly River's Famous Joe Cosley.

---

[85] First published in the Canadian Cattlemen, August and September of 1953 issues.

CHAPTER 22

CANADIAN TRAPPER PRETENDER

(Written but not signed by a second trapping partner of Joe Cosley)

This is the story of how I became enamored with furs.

I live in Cardston, Alberta in Canada and times were getting tougher. In the mid 1920's times were very rough on me and my wife and kid. I had lots of work during the spring and summer months and even into the fall. What I needed was a second job that provided me money for the winter. That way I would have the money to make it well past Christmas before my regular job started paying again.

And so it was in Cardston where I had the fortune, or to put it bluntly, the misfortune of meeting my trapping partner for the coming winter of 1927-28. For obvious reasons I will not mention my name. I don't want any of my family to find out. However, I will concede that my new business partner was a real mountain man and a tough individual. After I was associated with him and I learned what I know now, I didn't want to be associated with him any more.

This story is really the experience of how I became, "The older I get, the better I used to be," as I will later reveal.

This sounds like I am bitter about the whole experience of the wilderness and I'm not. It was the start of a beautiful relationship with nature in the high mountains in Alberta. It is just that if I had it to live over again, I would not have done it.

I had longed for the life where I could live close with nature in our beautiful mountains. I wasn't planning to trap furs.

It was the famous Joe Cosley that fired me with the desire to become a wilderness trapper. Over the next few months I was indoctrinated into a long line of wilderness trappers. I had never trapped before nor had I handled the skins but Joe was an expert at all of it and he showed me how.

You would think that with Cosley being the expert and I the beginner that it would have been me that approached him and asked him to train me in this new profession. Not so. He being troubled with "the shorts," financially of course, I put up the dough for the provisions, etc., in exchange for his know-how of trapping mink, beaver, otter, fox and marten and the use of his traps.

I had known that Cosley was rich in the early summer when he sold his fur and then he was poor again a month or so later after spending all his money living "high on the hog."

All it took was for Cosley to ask me one day if I was earning enough money for the whole year. I said "no," and that started our partnership. But I didn't ever want to tell my family where I was going so they wouldn't find out.

Cosley didn't seem to want anyone to find that he was down near Mountain View either.

Cosley was determined to spend some time prospecting and he wanted me to go with him. I wanted to go to see what the trapping life would be like. I soon learned that prospecting is a pastime every trapper enjoys, especially when fur was as plentiful as it was this year.

If one's trapping ground can be thoroughly checked out in advance of the coming season, half the battle is won. I agreed to go on weekends, when I was off work and available, to ferret out runs and places suitable for making sets. In this manner we were able to ascertain just how many traps were needed for the two lines. We needed a few more traps and I bought them.

The days in the early fall were spent blacking and repairing traps and other equipment, as well as laying in a good supply of wood.

We dug and built two pits like a root cellar. Each was walled off complete with floor and ceilings. One of these caches was located through the floor on the upper cabin. We could walk and work on top of the door or we could lift the lid and go down the ladder to this room below.

The second location was an outside root cellar with a large door and walk-down stairs to the area below ground. Joe was taller and he could stand with clearance to spare.

The outside cavern was dry and secure against prevailing winds. I could imagine we would need part of one of these but didn't believe we would ever fill one. Each lid or door had a lock and both of us had a key.

The way I am writing this makes it sound like our cache areas were easy to make. On the contrary. We both dug with pick and shovel all weekend to build just one of these.

Cosley had a system, a routine, but this year, together, we were going to take a bigger share of prime fur and both of us would be the richer for getting together.

One trapline was three long loops of about 82 miles[86] total. Cosley said that in his best days he would handle a 200 mile circuit. I think he could have.

---

[86] Frank Goble states that they must have been trapping out of the Belly River Valley to have had a trapline of this length, and the fact that they caught so many Muskrats leads me to believe a good part of their line was out in the foothills.

We would have the high country trapping in the tall pines for marten and fox of three colors (red, silver and cross). Then descending into two different basins, we had a chain of lakes where mink and beaver and otter were plentiful. Muskrats were all over the place this year.

Cosley's trapline was longer than mine because he could snowshoe at the run and he worked faster managing each trap.

As Cosley didn't have enough trapline shelters we then started building these. Our line consisted of two trapper cabins and five shelters. We didn't plan to use all the shelters but some were built just in case we were caught by storm and couldn't make it back to camp and had to lay over.

Joe said we were finally ready.

Then on November 23 the snows came. This winter, as the old-timers will remember, was a real dilly. We had done some trapping before the snow but the real trapping started afterwards.

Our daily routine was to get an early start and be ready to run our spur trapline by 8 o'clock in the morning. When I use the words, "ready to run" our spur I am not kidding. Joe would strap on his snowshoes and he would be off at the full run and never stop until he arrived at the next set. He was tall and very strong at running. He said he had been on a trapline since he was a small kid in Ontario at the age of six.

Cosley still had his snowshoes from when he was a ranger. Mine were a little smaller but still of the pickerel type like Cosley's.

I went with Cosley on these spurs for a few days to learn the ropes. Cosley had to "run" slower for me to go with him. Then Cosley wanted me to try my hand at going alone. I didn't catch as many as Cosley did. It took me longer to dig out my traps and some of my catches got away. Then, that night we would return to the cabin together or meet back at the cabin as soon as we each could to prepare the skins. I told my failures and Joe had suggestions.

I cooked the meals. I could tell you a whole story about why.

When I was on my own, I usually found Joe back at the camp working on the skins that he had caught that day. He must have been back several hours before me because he always had many pelts already done up. And Cosley had caught more furs too. But I was still learning.

The remainder of the winter was spent digging traps out of deep snow and snowshoeing endless miles from home base to three side camps. I now knew what to do on my line and Cosley would leave to work his own. At times I would not see Cosley for a week at a time. Those were times that Cosley did not out trap me. Some weeks I even had more than he did. The following year I learned where Cosley's line was. I'll tell you all about it later.

I had no idea of how many steps there were to trapping animals. Our 'rat catch exceeded our expectations as did the mink. Catches this large represent a vast amount of work because if fur isn't properly stretched and fleshed, much of the profit will be lost. Gleaning the fur is only a small part of the actual work involved, and is where the fun stops and the work begins as Cosley always said over and over.

We worked into the night every night. We laboriously skinned and stretched every single 'rat and mink before hitting the sack.

He told stories -- some I didn't think were true, other I knew to be false and lies -- but not total lies. He seemed to always include some foundation of truth.

Cosley talked while he worked on the pelts at night. He knew a lot of people around Cardston, Mountain View, Beazer and Waterton. And he knew people in Glacier and other places across the line like Babb, Belton, Kalispell and Columbia.

I returned home to my family for the holidays with my share of the money for the catch of over 450 muskrats, 27 mink, lots of badger and coyotes were ready for the market. Rats were low in price but I still got a dollar and a quarter per pelt. Coyotes were four and a half to six dollars. Mink were in fair demand and I received a flat price of eight dollars each. Well worth my efforts. I had never been so rich, especially in December.

However, I didn't tell my family that my trapping partner was Joe Cosely. I wasn't ready to tell them.

It was our arrangement that starting out I would get one third of the profits of the venture. Cosley had the know-how and he could trap more than I could. Cosley also knew how to put the furs up real fine. So in a way I was paying for Cosley's skill and experience to train me and the use of his traps.

Cosley and I agreed to take a break until the weather warmed up to 10° below zero. That turned out to be all of January and February. It was the middle of March before we resumed.

Even though it had snowed several times during January and February, when we returned to our traplines it looked like under the most recent snow there were snowshoe tracks. I could see tracks, not mine, and the fresh snow only compacted a few inches instead of a foot.

Somebody had been working my line. However, my traps were still pulled and stored in the cabin and clean. Cosley said I was mistaken and we needed to get to work fast and that was that.

Now I was working like a beaver to catch as many animals of all types and get the fur ready for market. My legs could hold up at faster speeds and I really covered more ground. But not like Joe could. He could out snowshoe me both in speed and distance and still have the reserve to do it again or go further distances. Some of the stories I have heard about how Joe Cosley could snowshoe 40 to 50 miles a day were very modest.

I caught more animals now, could work faster to put them up and I was really contributing to the partnership. However, I could never sustain the pace Cosley could.

Before we returned to trapping in late February Cosley agreed that my share should be worth half our pelts. That made me work even harder than before.

I was sure glad we had taken the time to get our fuel stored in our camps in the fall. With the heavy snows there would have been no way to have dug out windfall or deadfall. Even though I was lonely for my wife and family I was kept busy with getting my furs ready for market, which meant a cash crop to me. I loved the cash crop that it meant to me.

We made good use of our cache areas.

The beaver we caught was a record. Even Cosley had not seen such a great year. As we worked we talked to better plans for next year. Going in to this venture I had only planned on working with Cosley for one winter. However, since we were so successful and could work together, which took some doing, I decided to go it again next season.

Beaver were our real cash crop. The pelts were prime. Cosley continued to get more for his pelts than what mine brought. It was the way Joe prepared and put up his fur that brought the higher price. Prime beaver blankets brought us between $36 and $71 dollars. We had lots of extra large blankets.

The most I ever received was $52 but Cosley got lots of $70 and $71 prices. I was now working in town for the summer and home with my family every night.

We had both agreed we would not tell any others that we were partners. However, some stories got back to me that Cosley had said that he and I were trapping together. I just laughed it off that Cosley was exaggerating like he does and nothing more was said.

Joe Cosley was still "short" the next fall and needed me to grub stake our trapping. Cosley didn't even have enough money to live on for food. He had been bumming around his friends for the summer months and had worn out his welcome I guess.

Now for the next year. We had scouted out an even larger double trapline. After much hard work we were ready for the trapping season to start. This is when I started noticing again some things that Cosley was doing that I couldn't explain and he never told me.

Over our first season together there were things that just didn't add up to me. Now, there were more unusual events that concerned me and our arrangement. Not any single event was anything to wonder about but when added up there was something wrong with the answers and the facts.

It was more than just Cosley's eating habits that made me sick to my stomach some times. It was his way of living. He lived like a pig. He never cleaned up after himself and the floor was where almost everything he had seemed to belong.

Cosley was a private person who liked to keep to himself, especially in the mountains. Joe didn't like the idea of anyone knowing what he was doing at any time or where he was doing it. He was hard to find if I was looking for him. And yet I had found tracks that I later discovered paralleled mine for miles as if he was following me.

We both had different snowshoes and his pace was much greater than mine. One time I was following a weasel track when I first came across Joe's tracks. I was so surprised I thought something must have happened to him. I later asked him about the situation and he seemed to make something up. At the time I found his tracks I followed them following me a previous time for two miles and then his trail turned south into Waterton Park. He said I was mistaken and maybe snow crazy.

I know what I saw. A slash is a slash. I did not have time or the inclination to follow Joe's tracks into Waterton National Park.

The second year, before it snowed, Joe wanted me to go and check on the beaver dam near West's. Then he wanted me to prospect to the east of there and south. He gave me his .22 rifle and asked me to bring back a rabbit for supper. Joe was going north down stream to look at game signs there and then cross over the river and go further west to the Waterton. We were to meet back at camp at sundown.

We parted. I checked on the beaver dam and stayed on the east side of the river and hiked up the Lee Ridge going east and south. What a grand Indian Summer that fall. From the slash on this hill looking west I spotted Joe running straight south. He was either on the Blood Indian land or Waterton Park and it looked like he was running down the old wagon road. What was he doing this far south and what was he doing headed south on the old wagon road?

When Cosley returned to camp I questioned him. He used some excuse that I was mistaken. I was not. Cosley glared at me and I pushed it this time and he changed his tune.

It turned out that Cosley admitted that he had been trapping in Waterton and Glacier Parks since he arrived in the west in the early

1890's. His trapping lines were established long before these parks were made into parks by governments down east. Cosley was there first and, in his mind, that is the last of it. He will continue to trap there forever.

I told Joe that I did not want to trap in the parks.

He asked me where I thought all his furs the previous season had come from. They had come from Glacier and Waterton Park areas.

I said I was worried about being caught by either the Waterton Wardens or Glacier Rangers and be arrested and tried as a criminal.

Cosley responded that the new ranger for Belly River was just a kid and the one for Waterton was too fat to ever catch us. Then he put a dollar amount to the furs from Glacier and Waterton and asked me if I could have got by without my share of those pelts. Well, now that he put it that way, I could not have I was sorry to admit.

Joe continued to point out facts about the two parks. Joe said he knew the patrols of both the ranger and the warden in the parks and that they both lived and worked like clockwork. Joe said he knew exactly where they would be at all times. He said we could easily avoid those two yahoos.

Joe got upset as he spoke about Glacier and raised his voice. It was the only time he did.

He told me that it was time for me to choose sides, that he had taken a risk on me, he had taught me how to trap and now I knew his ways. Joe asked, "Are you a friend or an enemy?" I said, "You are a friend." That was the end of it.

But that was not the end of it. I still knew I would be breaking the law on both sides of the line and I felt bad about doing that.

I would have more to feel bad about very soon.

The next day Joe and I went into his trapping area in Glacier National Park to check it out. Cosley had been to part of his trapline and wanted me to join him in finishing prospecting there. We packed enough for three days (two days in Glacier and one in Waterton on the way out).

At the end of the second day, I was caught crossing the old wagon road by the U. S. Ranger, Heimes. He was not a kid. Heimes put the fear of God into me. He ran me down with his horse. The ranger jumped off his horse, grabbed me, and took my rifle away. The rifle was actually Joe's and I thought I was in real trouble.

Joe was a whole day out of when the "young ranger kid" goes to get his mail.

I was in double trouble. I was caught by ranger Heimes and Cosley's rifle had been taken from me. I thought I was going to be arrested by the ranger and shot by Cosley for losing his trusty 22 rifle.

Heimes pumped the shells out of the rifle as he pumped me with questions on what I was doing in the park with a loaded rifle. He shouted and I gave as few answers as I could think of. The ranger knew I was in the park poaching or what else would I be doing there with a rifle.

He asked my name and where I was from. He asked if I had a permit to be in the park. He asked what I was going to do in jail after I was arrested and tried for poaching in a national park. He asked who I was working with. He even asked if I was working with Joe Cosley. The questioning seemed unending. I didn't tell him very much.

Ranger Heimes didn't need a loaded rifle to kill me. He could cut me to pieces with his questions and his eyes.

I felt bad about breaking the law. I was raised better. I knew better. I was wrong and I was guilty. I told the ranger that and he seemed to settle down.

He told me to never come back into Glacier Park again, especially to Belly River. He told me he would arrest me next time and take me in to jail and the court would throw the key away. He asked if I understood. I did.

Then he really surprised me. He gave the .22 rifle back to me and told me to run out of the park just as fast as I could. I did.

Two years later I sat down in my private moments and wrote those experiences by hand as part of my determination to never do anything like this again. It was wrong of me to break the law and I was probably lucky to have been stopped by just one of the parks.

I was doubly lucky. If I had had my pack with me containing my traps or furs inside I would be in jail and I know it.

I was so grateful to have been let go after being caught in the park. I feel I must forever repent over this and so this written story of mine.

I still don't want to put my name on this and I don't ever want my wife and children to find out how bad I have been and how low my moral behavior has been.

To end the story, I met Cosley in Cardston a week later after I didn't show up at the camp. He wanted his rifle and to know why I didn't bring back a rabbit or fool-hen to camp. I wanted to keep his rifle until Cosley paid me for me "grubstaking" him for this year's trapping. I told him I was finished with trapping with him.

In the end I took pity on Joe and returned the rifle to him.

I never saw any of my money that I put up for Cosley's food and supplies until I threatened him. He told me that since I did not trap, I would not get any money back. He said it was all or nothing. I told him that I would go to the newspaper and tell them the truth about the famous Joe Cosley and his trapping in Waterton and Glacier National

Parks. He gave me the money right then and threatened to kill me if I ever told on him. I knew he meant it.

In the end I was glad I was not arrested and taken to trial. If I had been arrested and tried I knew I would not have been as lucky as Cosley getting out so fast after trial.

I have not trapped to this day.

I hope my resolves can be part of my repentance to change my life to the kind I want to live and be known for. I don't want to be known as a law breaker in or out of the park.

In the end, I wouldn't trade my life for Joe Cosley's for anything. He tells stories that are not exactly the truth. He is clever and inventive and his stories held my attention but he wasn't square with me.

I thought I was finished with my letter. Actually I was finished but the story did not end when I finished writing.

Later I learned Cosley had sold many furs to a rich city man who would drive to Mountain View and meet Cosley. They would strike a deal and Cosley was paid well. The furs Cosley sold the city dude were unaccounted for in our partnership. Cosley didn't tell me about these and we didn't split them. Cosley hid them from me. I also learned that Cosley sold two black beaver pelts that brought him the highest rate ever to these parts. I trust the person who saw those pelts and then told me.

A year ago, Cosley publicized that he was arrested in Alberta and taken to trial in Glacier Park against his will. Cosley finally escaped and ran back to recover his cache of furs. I felt that only a small part of his story to the newspaper was true. Cosley was the hero over this race after his get-away from jail but I think the whole story has not been told.

Several weeks later I saw the same U. S. ranger from Glacier, that ran me down with his horse and questioned me, he was in Cardston. I later learned that this Heimes fellow from Glacier stood up to Cosley and Cosley never said another word to him -- just walked off fast. This happened to me when I stood up to Cosley and when I trapped Cosley in a lie, he did not want to talk about it.

I think the U. S. ranger also knows Cosley for who he is. A year afterwards I talked to Joe Cosley or rather he came to talk to me. He said he had been up in the north country and found solitude. He had returned to Cardston to get his traps and mountain gear, then he was going back up north where the trapping was prime.

He wanted to offer me an exclusive to invest in his venture and put up the grubstake. Rather than just say, "no," I asked him about all the furs he had sold to a man from Lethbridge back when Joe and I were "partners."

Joe said the stories about him were all lies including maybe this one. However, he was silent after I told him that the man had backed up this account.

Then I had several questions and statements that I wanted to get off my chest and clear the air. "Is this the way you lie to your former partner?" "Is this the way you treat me, to steal furs from me?" Joe just walked away and never replied to my questions. He left as if he was moving like he snowshoes on the traplines.

I had more that I wanted to say to Joe but he was gone in almost a flash and was out of my life. I wanted to say something about the black pelts he sold the season we were together. I was just glad I didn't give him any money.

I will never enter into another partnership.

I heard from two others in town that Cosley had been to them first and offered each of them a deal that was too good to turn down. They both turned down Joe's offer. The one had no money and said so. The other had money and was aware that any person in partnership with the famous Cosley was sure to come up with the short end.

I am determined to never do anything illegal again. That is my conviction. At the same time, I still find myself thinking about the times I had with Joe Cosley up in the trapping fields. He was good. He was the best I have ever seen or heard about. I could never keep up with him.

Part of me wishes Joe well up north. He is the last of a kind. I hope he is able to catch some more black beaver.

I have forgiven Joe for not being equal with me in our partnership deal. I just want the matter to end and be resolved in my heart. I am still concerned that it may not be resolved in my soul.

At the same time, part of me wants to hear another exciting experience of Joe's.

{Unsigned}

Canadian Trapper Pretender, Statement from Brian McClung

I was thrilled to find this letter about trapping with Joe Cosley. Even though I had to promise, before I could see this letter, that I would never reveal who wrote this message or which family name was involved, I believed that receiving this letter would be worth it. And it was.

CHAPTER 23

PRESERVING THE JOE COSLEY STORY

Persons interested in learning more about Joe Cosley may contact: Cardston and District Historical Society (Dave Edmonds) at 403-653-3744, Waterton Natural History Association at 403-859-2624, First Best Place Task Force at 406-250-6100 or the N.W. Montana Historical Society - Museum at Central School 406-756-8381

Cosley Tree Still Living and Standing Tall in Waterton Park

What an historical find.

Joe Cosley carved trees everywhere he went: Ontario, Northern Alberta and Saskatchewan. Thousands of early hikers and campers to Glacier and Waterton have seen Cosley Trees. One aspen tree upon which Cosley carved his name and the date is still living. It is located in Waterton Park. Can you imagine how old this tree must be?

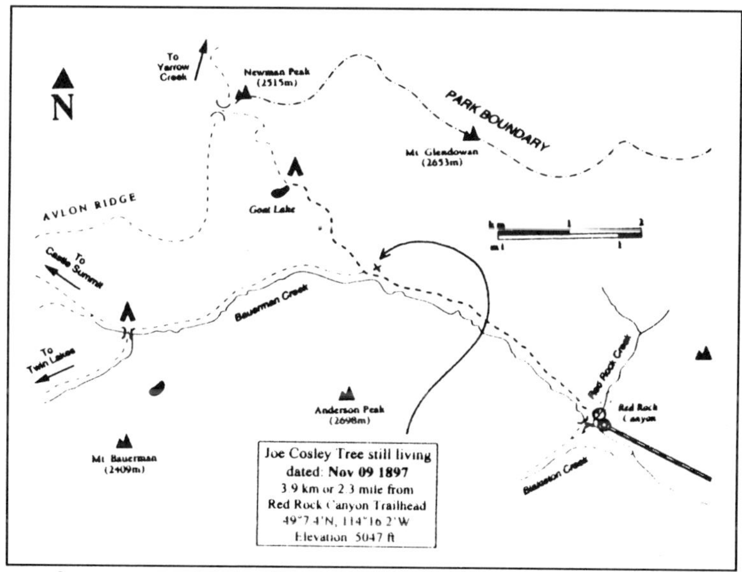

Map of Cosley Tree on Twin Lakes trail near junction with Goat Lake in Bauerman Valley west of Red Rock Canyon in Waterton Park.

Edwin describes the tree. "This tree is located in the Bauerman Valley west of Red Rock Canyon in Waterton Lakes National Park. The aspen tree is located in a grassy meadow on the north side (right side) of the trail. This clearing is the first of any significance approximately 300 meters east of the Goat Lake Junction. A hedge of tall young spruce-fir trees grows in the old road ditch between the trail and the meadow. The Cosley Tree stands alone in the center of this meadow about 30 feet from the trail. The tree is approximately 80 feet tall and 18" in diameter. The carving is about six feet above the ground."

Edwin Knox and his dog "Cosley" at the Cosley Tree near Goat Lake Junction on the Snowshoe Trail in Bauerman Valley, west of Red Rock.
Photo by Rebecca Rothgeb

"The tree is an unusual specimen of an aspen tree. There is a lot of life still in it and the upper branches are thick. There are numerous other names, dates carved. Above, there is a large bold arrow inscribed in the tree."

Important Find

There aren't very many Cosley Trees left.

When I was a kid I could name the exact spots of dozens of Cosley carved trees. However, over the years, the trail has changed. Storms have downed some of the older dated carvings.

Edwin Knox studying the Cosley inscription, Joe Cosley, Nov 09, 1897, just above Edwin's left hand, still readable after more than a century. Notice other carvings also. Photo by Rebecca Rothgeb.

Today, I wouldn't be able to name one location. On all my recent trips into the backcountry I have looked, and I didn't see any of Joe Cosley's Trees.

That makes this discovery even more important to me.

Another Historic Find

A saddle, once owned by Joe Cosley, has been located in Cardston. Joe Cosley used this saddle on his favorite horse "Vassar." Joe was not only a fancy rider but also a fancy outfitter. "The elegance of his pack outfits — alligator leather on the saddles, silver-mounted spurs and bridles, impressed them."[87]

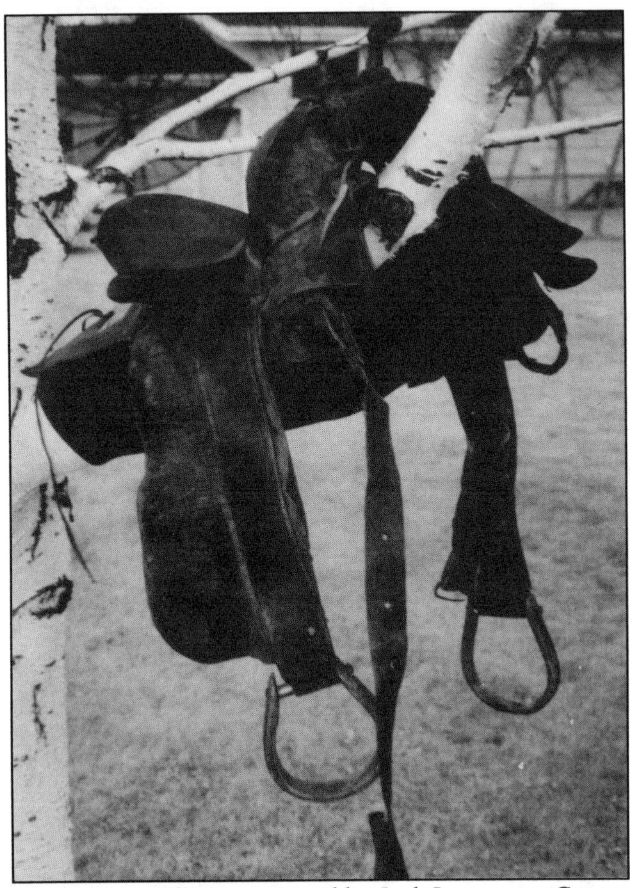

Joe Cosley's former saddle, now owned by Jack Lowe near Carway, Alberta
Notice the alligator hide tooling look of this saddle
Photo courtesy of Edwin Knox, 1998

Well, it wasn't alligator leather but alligator "stamp" which was just steer hide "stamped" or tooled to look like alligator leather. Even after all these years you can still see for yourself that this saddle of Joe's has alligator stamping.

---

[87] Roots and Branches, "History of Mountain View"

Here's the story.

In the autumn of 1997 Edwin Knox stopped into Doug Hall's Saddlery and Harness Shop in Cardston.

Knox continues. "Doug was building a nice breast collar - back pad harness for my Golden Retriever who's name is "Cosley."

"I asked Doug if he knew of the Cosley name? It didn't twig right away with him but then Doug started to talk about a character and, of course, it was Cosley who he was talking about. Doug related about the poaching incident in Belly River, etc.

"I continued to tell Doug about the supposedly fairly fancy tack Cosley had for his horse and that one saddle was said to have been made out of alligator hide.

Approximately 100 year old "Frazier Saddle" once owned by Joe Cosley, now owned by Jack Lowe, Granite Ranch near Carway, Alberta. Notice the alligator hide tooling look on the saddlebow. Photo courtesy of Edwin Knox, 1998

"So Doug Hall says, "Well, low and behold. You wouldn't believe what I have in the attic of my garage." He sent his son up into the attic and the son hands down this old saddle. On first appearance, indeed, it is alligator hide or crocodile leather.

"So Doug continued. 'This saddle is reputed to have belonged to Joe Cosley.' The saddle was made in Pueblo, Colorado by R. T. Frazier.'

"I set the saddle on a limb of a tree and took some pictures.

"So, this saddle matches the story I have read about Joe Cosley and it is quite interesting," states Knox.

Joe Cosley sold his saddle to Leo Lowe shortly after losing his horses while crossing Ahern Pass in 1929. The Lowe family used this saddle for many years. As a boy, Jack Lowe remembers riding on the saddle and knows every unique part of it.

Stirrup of Joe Cosley's famous fancy saddle,
made in Pueblo, Colorado by the R. T. Frazier Saddlery Company.
The alligator hide tooling still looks impressive after all these years.
Owned by Jack Lowe, Granite Ranch, Cardston, Alberta.
Photo courtesy of Edwin Knox, 1998

The Cosley Collection

The Joe Cosley Museum has found a great home with the First Best Place Task Force and the Glacier Discovery Center in Columbia Falls, Montana. This community based, non-profit organization is partnered with the Northwest Montana Historical Society and the Museum at Central School in Kalispell, Montana. They are also mentored by Glacier National Park historians to assure professional protocol and care in handling The Cosley Collection.

We have tracked down artifacts from the life of Joe Cosley and most of the owners have agreed to lend or donate their Cosley treasurers:

ITEMS IDENTIFIED AS OF SPRING 2009

1. Cosley Saddle owned by Jack Lowe
2. Cosley Original Art "RIDE 'EM STRAIGHT UP", given by Dee Kenly to his friend Jack Lowe (see page 9 of this book.)
3. Cosley Post Card Collection and photographs owned by Richard West
4. Cosley Traps owned by Terry Nelson
5. Joe's Métis Sash inherited by a member of the Causley family.
Cosley Original Art "THE WILD HORSE BUCKAROO", given by Dee Kenly to his niece NaVeda Lewis.(see page 24 of this book)
6. Cosley Carved Tree
7. Cosley Poetry
8. Cosley Articles
9. Cosley Traps
10. Cosley Diary

It would be wonderful to find the trunk full of art, drawings, sketches, articles and diaries that belonged to Joe Cosley. Marie and I hope that Joe's friends and family will phone us at 702-360-8162, if they have any information or Cosley treasures

The display area for The Cosley Collection will be complete and ready on May 11, 2010 to celebrate Glacier National Park's Centennial in Joe Cosley style! Not wanting to compete with Glacier National Park's Official Centennial activities, The Cosley Collection Official Unveiling will take place on Saturday, July 24, 2010. The Mountain Man Rendezvous (Cosley Camp) will take place on the same day. These events will be a spectacular celebration of Glacier National Park's Centennial and the Famous Joe Cosley.

APPENDIX #1

BELLY RIVER Fraternity of Rangers with Joe Cosley as Chairman

YEAR	RANGER (S) COMMENTS
1910	Joseph Cosley
1911	Joseph Cosley
1912	Joseph Cosley
1913	Joseph Cosley
	Harry Reynolds (1-2), Barn, Old Station
1914	Joseph Cosley (1-6) Fired for poaching, large sale of furs. He was never caught poaching or trapping but still fired. No more Glacier Park paychecks for Cosley.
	Cosley joined Canadian army in August in Cardston.
1915	
1916	
1917	
1918	M. R. Cooper
1919	M. R. Cooper
1920	M. R. Cooper
1921	H. C. Hockett
1922	H. C. Hockett
1923	H. C. Hockett
1924	H. C. Hockett
1925	H. C. Hockett
	Joseph F. Heimes arrived Dec. 5
	Joseph F. Heimes also on Huckleberry
	New Station started in 1925 but not finished
1926	Joseph F. Heimes, Joe Heimes also in Kishenehn. BR Ranger Station was not worked on because of forest fire on west side (Flathead River Valley)
1927	Joseph F. Heimes, New station finished at BR
	Old station used for storage and later work shop
1928	Joseph F. Heimes
1929	Joseph F. Heimes
	Clarence Willey (10-12)
1930	Clarence Willey (1-6)
	Hilbert O. Krause
1931	Hilbert O. Krause
1932	Hilbert O. Krause (1-6)
	Elmer Ness (6-12)
1933	Elmer Ness
	Elmer Fladmark
	Burt Edwards
	Elmer Ness injured Dec. 1933
1934	Elmer Fladmark (1-4)
	Elmer Ness (4-10)
	Andy Fleutsch (10-12)
1935	Andy Fleutsch
1936	Andy Fleutsch
1937	Andy Fleutsch

1938	Joseph F. Heimes
1939	Joseph F. Heimes
	John C. Lindahl (10-12)
1940	John C. Lindahl
1941	Joseph F. Heimes
1942	Joseph F. Heimes (1-10)
1943	Joseph F. Heimes
1944	Joseph F. Heimes
1945	Clem J. Harner
1946	Joseph F. Heimes
1947	Joseph F. Heimes, Last year of "Year Around" at BR
1948	Joseph F. Heimes, May 18 to October 3
1949	Joseph F. Heimes, June 1 to September 30
1950	Joseph F. Heimes, June 2 to September 30
1951	Joseph F. Heimes, June 8 to September 30
1952	Joseph F. Heimes, May 10 to September 30
1953	Joseph F. Heimes, May 18 to September 30
1954	Edward P. Olmstead, May 27 to September 30
1955	Edward P. Olmstead, May 13 to September 30
1956	Edward P. Olmstead, May 21 to October 12
1957	Joseph F. Heimes, May 15 to October 11
1958	Joseph F. Heimes, June 3 to October 4
1959	Joseph F. Heimes, May 28 to September 30
1960	Joseph F. Heimes
	R. L. Fitzpatrick, June 1 to September 30
1961	Joseph F. Heimes, June 1st. to September 30.
	Last year a Jeep and Wagon team entered BR
1962	Lou Hendricks, June 1st. to September 30
1963	Lou Hendricks, April to October 2nd.
1964	Fred Wood
1965	Fred Wood
1966	Jerome (Jerry) S. De Santo Wrote on Joe Cosley
1967	Edward P. Olmstead
1968	Edward P. Olmstead
1969	Edward P. Olmstead
1970	Tom Whalan, April to October
1971	Curt Miller, April to October
1972	Tom Whalan, April to October
1973	Kerel Hagen, April to October
1974	Kerel Hagen
	Dave Shea, April to October
1975	David and Ruth Shea, April to October
1976	David and Ruth Shea, April to October
1977	David Shea
	Ernest Lommatsch, April to October
1978	David Shea, April to October
1979	Ernest Lommatsch, April to October
1980	Ernest Lommatsch, April to October
1981	Mark Oltman, April to October
1982	Mark Oltman, April to October
1983	David Shea, April to October

1984	David Shea, April to October
1985	David Shea, April to October
1986	David Shea, April to October
1987	David Shea, April to October
1988	David Shea Wrote about Joe Cosley and Belly River
	Chuck Cameron, April to October
1989	Chuck Cameron, (seasonal)
1990	Chuck Cameron, (seasonal)
1991	Chuck Cameron, (seasonal)
1992	Chuck Cameron, (seasonal)
1993	Chuck Cameron, (seasonal)
1994	Chuck Cameron, (seasonal)
1995	Chuck Cameron, (seasonal)
1996	Chuck Cameron, (seasonal)
1997	Steve Prather, (seasonal)
1998	Steve Prather, (seasonal)
1999	
2000	
2001	
2002	
2003	
2004	
2005	
2006	
2007	
2008	
2009	
2010	

Joseph F. Heimes	= 26 years were in Belly River. = he worked in GNP 38 years.
David Shea	= 11 years, all were seasonal
Chuck Cameron	= 9 years, all seasonal
Edward P. Olmstead	= 6 years, all year long
H. C. Hockett	= 5 years, all year long, drunk all the time, out of park most of the time.
Joe C. Cosley	= 5 years, all year long, but he was usually not there

APPENDIX #2

BELLY RIVER TRAVEL REPORT (Sampling only)

Records not complete. Started in 1923 and periodic months or years were missed.

1923 Ranger: H. C. Hockett

DATE	NAME	ADDRESS	TRANSPORTATION
June 28	J. B. Scott	Waterton Park, Canada	Team & Wagon
	Quinton Leginch	Waterton Park, Canada	Team & Wagon
July 4	A.G. State	Mountain View, Alberta	Team & Wagon
	J. S. Webster	Mountain View, Alberta	Team & Wagon
July 8	John J. West	Mountain View, Alberta	Team & Wagon
	John W. Webster	Mountain View, Alberta	Team & Wagon
July 13	John J. West	Mountain View, Alberta	Saddle Horse
	John W. Webster	Mountain View, Alberta	Saddle Horse

* * *

1924 Ranger: H. C. Hockett

DATE	NAME	ADDRESS	TRANSPORTATION
July 1	John McNeil	White Plans N. Y.	Saddle Horse
	Miss Pearl Moir	Cardston, Alberta	Saddle Horse
	Miss Thelma Cahoon	Cardston, Alberta	Saddle Horse
	Kenneth Scott	Cardston, Alberta	Saddle Horse
	Mrs. M. Ivins	Cardston, Alberta	Saddle Horse
	R. Mackenzie	Caldwell, Alberta	Team and Wagon
	A. G. Strate	Mountain View, Alberta	Team and Wagon
	Grant Laidlaw	Mountain View, Alberta	Team and Wagon
	J. G. Webster	Mountain View, Alberta	Team and Wagon
	J. J. West	Mountain View, Alberta	Team and Wagon
July 18	Norman Webster	Glenwood, Alberta	Saddle Horse
August 24	Mrs. Webster	Cardston, Alberta	Team & Wagon
	Mr. Webster	Cardston, Alberta	Team & Wagon

* * *

1925 Ranger: H. C. Hockett

DATE	NAME	ADDRESS	TRANSPORTATION
August 18	Mrs. K. Chipps	Boundary Creek, Alberta	Pack Horse
	Mrs. A. Scott	Boundary Creek, Alberta	Team and Wagon
	Mr. A. Scott	Boundary Creek, Alberta	Team and Wagon
	Mr. & Mrs. B. Webster	Salt Lake City, Utah	Pack Horse
	F. Webster	Mountain View, Alberta	Pack Horse
August 20	Mrs. Ivins	Cardston, Alberta	Saddle Horse
	Miss Creed	Cardston, Alberta	Saddle Horse
	Jack Moir	Cardston, Alberta	Saddle Horse
Sept.	E. J. Ivins	Cardston, Alberta	Team and Wagon
	E. Ivins Jr.	Cardston, Alberta	Team and Wagon

* * *

1927 Ranger: Joe Heimes

DATE	NAME	ADDRESS	TRANSPORTATION
July 4	Frank McKeague	Waterton Park, Can.	Saddle Horse
	N. R. McKeague	Chesty, Nova Scotia	Saddle Horse

August 9	John J. West	Mountain View, Alberta	Team and Wagon
	Cliff Nerville	Mountain View, Alberta	Team and Wagon
	C. M. Blair	Belton, Montana	Team & Wagon
	Edward J. Auger	Belton, Montana	Team & Wagon
	Mr. Chapman	Columbia Falls, Montana	Team & Wagon
	Mrs. Chapman	Columbia Falls, Montana	Team & Wagon
Sept. 24	Dorothy Selby	Boundary Creek, Alberta	Saddle Horse
	Mrs. K. Chipps	Boundary Creek, Alberta	Saddle Horse
	Majorie Cheney	Boundary Creek, Alberta	Saddle Horse

* * *

1928 Ranger: Joe Heimes

DATE	NAME	ADDRESS	TRANSPORTATION
May 25	Mrs. Margaret Ivins	Cardston, Alberta	Saddle Horse
	Charlie Ivins	Cardston, Alberta	Saddle Horse
	Eddie Ivins	Beazer, Alberta	Saddle Horse
June 1	Mrs. K. Chipps	Boundary Creek, Alta.	Saddle Horse
	Miss Marjorie Cheney	Boundary Creek, Alta.	Saddle Horse
June 11	Alroy West	Mountain View, Alberta	Saddle Horse
	Percy Kelley	Valeer, Montana	Saddle Horse
June 12	Bert Barnes	Waterton Park Belly River	Saddle Horse
	Mrs. Barnes	Waterton Park Belly River	Saddle Horse
July 9	J. J. West	Mountain View, Alberta	Team and Wagon
	Mrs. J. J. West	Mountain View, Alberta	Team and Wagon
	Miss Renee West	Mountain View, Alberta	Saddle Horse
	Mr. Norris West	Mountain View, Alberta	Saddle Horse
July 10	Al Thompson	Mountain View, Alberta	Team and Wagon
	Oakley Thompson	Mountain View, Alberta	Team and Wagon
	Trevor Thompson	Mountain View, Alberta	Saddle Horse
	Roy Bash	Boundary Creek, Alberta	Saddle Horse
July 14	Burt Strate	Mountain View, Alberta	Team and Wagon
	Al Strate	Waterton Park, Alberta	Team and Wagon
July 28	Mrs. Al Thompson	Mountain View, Alberta	Team and Wagon
	Vaughn Thompson	Mountain View, Alberta	Team and Wagon
	C. Thompson	Mountain View, Alberta	Team and Wagon
August 21	L. S. McAlister	Waterton Park, Alberta	Saddle Horse
	David Carmarty	Waterton Park, Alberta	Saddle Horse
August 24	Miss Mary Elhert	Beazer, Alberta	Saddle Horse
	Miss Vera Walburger	Leavitt, Alberta	Saddle Horse
	Miss Bertha Elhert	Magrath, Alberta	Saddle Horse
	Miss Amy Broadhead	Leavitt, Alberta	Saddle Horse
	Miss Ellen Cahoon	Leavitt, Alberta	Saddle Horse
	Miss Clarice Williams	Leavitt, Alberta	Saddle Horse
Sept. 27	Nellie Hunter	Waterton Park	Saddle Horse

* * *

1929 Ranger: Joe Heimes

DATE	NAME	ADDRESS	TRANSPORTATION
June 12	Mrs. Channing Howell	Kennedy Creek Station	Saddle Horse
	Miss Estella Isackson	Two Harbors, Minn.	Saddle Horse
June 15	Miss Della Findley	Mountain View, Alberta	Saddle Horse
	Mrs. K. Chipps	Boundary Creek, Alta.	Saddle Horse

June 19	John J. West	Mountain View, Alberta	Team and Wagon
June 30	Mr. Burt Strate	Mountain View, Alberta	Saddle Horse
July 1	Travor Thompson	Mountain View, Alberta	Saddle Horse
	Aaron Thompson	Mountain View, Alberta	Saddle Horse
July 5	Dorothy Barnes	Waterton Belly River Station	Saddle Horse
	Effie Barnes	Waterton Park, Alberta	Saddle Horse
July 10	Alroy West	Mountain View, Alberta	Saddle Horse
August 20	Mrs. K. Chipps	Boundary Creek, Alberta	Saddle Horse
	Frank Jessop	Boundary Creek, Alberta	Saddle Horse
	Miss Irine Jessop	Boundary Creek, Alberta	Saddle Horse
	George Jessop	Boundary Creek, Alberta	Saddle Horse
August 21	Mr. E. J. Ivins	Beazer, Alberta	Team and Wagon
	Mrs. E. Ivins	Cardston, Alberta	Team and Wagon
	Mr. Eddie Ivins	Cardston, Alberta	Saddle Horse
	Mr. Charlie Ivins	Cardston, Alberta	Saddle Horse
	Jack Moir	Cardston, Alberta	Saddle Horse
	Miss Baby Moir	Lethbridge, Alberta	Saddle Horse
	Miss Della Findley	Mountain View, Alberta	Saddle Horse
	Mrs. Lila Hicken	Cardston, Alberta	Saddle Horse

* * *

1930 Rangers: Clarence Willey (1-6), Hilbert O. Krause

DATE	NAME	ADDRESS	TRANSPORTATION
July 1	Dorothy Barnes	Waterton Park	
	____________ party 8		
Sept. 3	J. J. West	Mountain View, Alberta	Saddle Horse
	Mrs. J. J. West	Mountain View, Alberta	Saddle Horse
	Ree Nee West	Mountain View, Alberta	Saddle Horse
	Norris West	Mountain View, Alberta	Saddle Horse
	J. W. Webster	Mountain View, Alberta	Saddle Horse
	Mrs. J. W. Webster	Mountain View, Alberta	Saddle Horse
	Afton Webster	Mountain View, Alberta	Saddle Horse
Nov 11	E. D. Caldwell	Cardston, Alberta	Car
	J. S. Low	Caldwell, Alberta	Car
	C. B. Cheeseman	Cardston, Alberta	Car

* * *

1931 Ranger: Hilbert O. Krause

DATE	NAME	ADDRESS	TRANSPORTATION
June 4	T. J. Weatherly	Babb, Montana	Saddle Horse
	Gaffney	Babb, Montana	Saddle Horse
June 11	A. G. Strate	Mountain View, Alberta	Team and Wagon
	J. S. Webster	Mountain View, Alberta	Team and Wagon
August 19	F. W. Flett	Waterton Lakes	Saddle Horse

* * *

1932 Ranger: Elmer Ness

DATE	NAME	ADDRESS	TRANSPORTATION
July 6	Hubert L. West	Mountain View, Alberta	Team & Wagon
	Naomi West	Mountain View, Alberta	Team & Wagon
	Ree Nee West	Mountain View, Alberta	Team & Wagon
July 7	Mrs. Morgan Strate	Mountain View, Alberta	Saddle Horse

Dec. 12	Burton Edwards	Glacier Park Station, Mont.	
	Chas. Petersen	Belton, Montana	

*   *   *

1933 Rangers: Elmer Ness (injured Dec. 1933), Elmer Fadmark, Burt Edwards

DATE	NAME	ADDRESS	TRANSPORTATION
July 3	Trevor Thompson	Mountain View, Alberta	Saddle Horse
	Park Strate	Mountain View, Alberta	Saddle Horse
	Authur Frederickson	Waterton Park	Saddle Horse
July 13	A. C. Strate	Mountain View, Alberta	Saddle Horse
	J. A. State	Hills Spring, Alberta	Saddle Horse
	J. F. Strate	Hills Spring, Alberta	Saddle Horse
August 9	Billie Webster	Mountain View, Alberta	Saddle Horse
	May Webster	Mountain View, Alberta	Saddle Horse

*   *   *

1934 Rangers: Elmer Fladmark (1-4), Elmer Ness (4-10), Andy Fleutsch (10-12)

DATE	NAME	ADDRESS	TRANSPORTATION
Sept. 1	B. D. Moss, Jr.	Burlington, Iowa	afoot
	Persh Gilligan	Topeka, Kansas	afoot
	John Turner	Conrad, Montana	afoot
Sept. 4	Mrs. O. A. Thompson	Mountain View, Alberta	Saddle Horse
	O. A. Thompson	Mountain View, Alberta	Saddle Horse

*   *   *

1944 Ranger: Joe Heimes

DATE	NAME	ADDRESS	TRANSPORTATION
August 19	Chief Warden Halroyd of Waterton Park		Saddle Horse
	Warden Christenson of Waterton Park		Saddle Horse
August 22	Gorden Christenson	Waterton Park	Saddle Horse
Sept. 11	Warden Christenson	Waterton Park	Saddle Horse
	Miss Mildred Christenson	Waterton Park	Saddle Horse

*   *   *

1945 Ranger: Clem Harner

DATE	NAME	ADDRESS	TRANSPORTATION
August 12	Park Naturalist Ed Beatty, Belton, Montana		Saddle Horse
	Charles Albert Harwell	Belton, Montana	Saddle Horse
	Ranger Adolph Opalka	U. S. W __________	Saddle Horse
Sept. 15	R. Christiensen	Can. Belly River Station	Saddle Horse
	C. R. Christiensen	Can. Belly River Station	Saddle Horse

*   *   *

1946 Ranger: Joe Heimes

DATE	NAME	ADDRESS	TRANSPORTATION
August 20	Clark Leaphart	(Park employee) St. Mary RS,	Car
	Bruce Miller	(Park employee) St. Mary RS	Car
August 21	M. Jacobs	Mountain View, Alberta	Saddle Horse
	June Webster	Mountain View, Alberta	Saddle Horse
	Fenton Webster	Mountain View, Alberta	Saddle Horse
	Luell Perrott	Mountain View, Alberta	Saddle Horse

*   *   *

1947 Ranger: Joe Heimes

DATE	NAME	ADDRESS	TRANSPORTATION
July 20	O. J. Weber	Waterton Lakes, Alberta	Foot
	M. G. Monjeune	Waterton Park, Alberta	Foot
July 24	E. N. Fladmark	Park hdq, Belton, Montana	Saddle Horse
	Bob Coonehy	Helena, Montana	Saddle Horse
	J. W. Leveny	Missoula, Montana	Saddle Horse
	A. A. O'Claire	Helena, Montana	Saddle Horse
	A. Grande	Lenny, Montana	Saddle Horse
	William Yenne	Park hdg, Belton, Montana	Saddle Horse
July 31	Grace A. Barnum	St. Marys	Car
	Ranger Don Barnum	St. Marys	Car
	J. B. Lindberg	St. Marys	Car
	Ray I. Terney	St. Marys	Car
	Ranger John F. Aiton	Park hdq, Belton, Montana	Foot
	Ranger George R. Hill	Park hdq, Belton, Montana	Foot
August 10	B. Davidson	Waterton, Alberta	Car
	O. W. Davidson	Waterton, Alberta	Car
August 12	W. G. Cappland	Sunburst, Montana	Foot
	H. R. Lawson	St. Marys	Foot
August 19	Duane Sammons	Cut Bank, Montana	Foot
	Duane Sammons Jr.	Cut Bank, Montana	Foot
	Darrel Crumley	Park Hdq. Belton, Montana	Foot
	"Whitey"	Belton, Montana	Foot
Sept. 6	Don Barnum	St. Mary	Saddle Horse
	Marvin Karrington	Many Glacier	Saddle Horse
	William J. Jenne	Belton Hdqtrs	Saddle Horse
	Bernice Lewis	Lewis ♦L Horses	Saddle Horse
	Patt Lewis	Lewis ♦L Horses	Saddle Horse
	Grace A. Barnum	St. Mary R. S.	Saddle Horse
Sept. 8	Edward F. O'Connell	Lewis ♦L Horses	Saddle Horse

* * *

1948 Ranger: Joe Heimes

DATE	NAME	ADDRESS	TRANSPORTATION
May 18	Joe F. Heimes	Glacier Park, Montana	Foot
June 11	C. W. Tran's	Coram, Montana	Pack String
	G. R. Poloson	St. Mary	Pack String
July 6	Bertha O'Connell	Lewis ♦L Horses	Saddle Horse
July 10	Fred I. Bussy	Glacier Nat'l Park, Belton	Foot
	David T. Baptlet	Glacier Nat'l Park, Belton	Foot
July 11	Richard K. Heuer	GPT Co. Kalamazoo, Mich.	Foot
	Carl A. Fitzgerald	GPT Co. Kinsville, Texas	Foot
July 12	Bertha O'Connell	Lewis ♦L Horses	Saddle Horse
	Shirley C. Ashley	Lewis ♦L Horses, Missoula	Saddle Horse
July 15	Ted Canfield	Lewis ♦L Horses, Browning	Saddle Horse
	James Pearcell	U. S. Customs, Sweetgrass, Montana	Foot
	Pat Sullivan	U. S. Customs, Spokane, Wash.	Foot
July 22	Shirley C. Ashley	Lewis ♦L Horses, Missoula	Saddle Horse
	W. R. Kelsey	Lewis ♦L Horses, Belton,	Saddle Horse

	Don Barnum	Dist. Ranger	
	Mrs. Bill Yenne		
	Bill Yenne	Packer	
	Mrs. Don Barnum		
August 2	Charles E. Syverson	Missoula Weather Dept.	Team & Wagon
August 25	Fred H. Poloson	Park Headquarters, Belton	
Sept. 6	Paul Janson	U. S. Border Patrol	
Sept. 8-9	Paul L. Webb	Over Ahern Pass, Belton	
	Jack Alton	Over Ahern Pass, Belton	
	R. A. Nelson	Over Ahern Pass, Belton	
	E. N. Fladmark	Over Ahern Pass, Belton	
Sept. 14	Ethel L. Meinzer	Park Headquarters	
	Don Barnum	St. Mary	
Sept. 29	Albert Poloson	St. Mary	
	Fred Poloson	Belton	
	Don Barnum	St. Mary	

1949 Ranger: Joe Heimes

DATE	NAME	ADDRESS	TRANSPORTATION
June 1	Joe Heimes	Glacier Park, Montana	Team and Wagon
	Bert Poloson	Glacier Park	Horse
	Lawrence Pogrebra	Box Elder, Montana	Horse
August 19	Morgan Strate	Mountain View, Alberta	Foot

* * *

1950 Ranger: Joe Heimes

DATE	NAME	ADDRESS	TRANSPORTATION
Sept. 9	G. L. Gladstone	Waterton B R Warden	Car
	Jim Sullivan	U. S. Immigration Dept.	Car
Sept. 11	Wallace Webster	Mountain View, Alberta	Saddle Horse
	Mr. and Mrs. Al Larson	U. S. Customs Dept.	Foot

* * *

1951 Ranger: Joe Heimes

DATE	NAME	ADDRESS	TRANSPORTATION
June 8	Joe F. Heimes	East Glacier, Montana	Team and Wagon
	Terrences A. McGuire	Fire Guard, San Francisco	Team and Wagon
August 1	Tom Mee	Baton Rouge, La	Parachute
	Rudy Stoll	St. Ignatius, Montana	Parachute
	Lee Rust Brown	Bloomingham, Ala.	Parachute
	Chas. Swain	Johnson City, Tennessee	Parachute
	Maxwell Starden	Deadwood, South Dakota	Parachute
	(the above men were U. S. Forest Service Smokejumpers based at Missoula, Montana, who jumped on a fire in this valley).		
Sept. 17	Robert Morris	U. S. Waterton RS	Pack Horse
	Marion Morris	U. S. Waterton RS,	Pack Horse

* * *

1952 Ranger: Joe Heimes

DATE	NAME	ADDRESS		TRANSPORTATION
Feb. 6-8	Hugh W. Buchanan	St. Mary RS	NPS	Snowshoes
	Bruce J. Miller	Shelburne RS	NPS	snowshoes
June 8	Joe F. Heimes	E. Glacier Park, Montana		Foot
	Chuck Bengtson	E. Glacier Park, Montana		Foot
June 10	Joe F. Heimes	East Glacier, Montana		Saddle Horse
	Chuck Bengtson	East Glacier, Montana		Saddle Horse
August 18	Dave Cannevina	NPS, West Glacier, Mont.		Iron Horse
	Nonbent J. Donalson	F. B. I, Kalispell, Mont.		Iron Horse
	A. Lynn Coffin	NPS West Glacier, Mont.		Iron Horse
Sept. 18	Marsha Gregg	Hungry Horse, Montana (Looks as beautiful as ever)		Foot
	Pat Stevenson	East Glacier Park		Foot
	Hazel Webb	East Glacier Park		Foot
	Leana Brown	East Glacier Park (caught 8 fish too		
Sept. 19	John Rybon	West Glacier		Foot

* * *

1953 Ranger Joe F. Heimes

DATE	NAME	ADDRESS	TRANSPORTATION
May 18	Joe F. Heimes	St. Mary	Team and Wagon
	Frank R. Hollopeter	St. Mary	Team and Wagon
July 22	Martha Hollopeter	Seeley Lake, Montana	Horse
	Mary Hollopeter	Seeley Lake, Montana	Horse
Aug 1	Fred Bussey	Chief Clerk, N.P.S.	West Glacier
	Clarke Bussey	West Glacier	
Aug 7	Herb Larsen	Ranger, St. Mary	
Sept 13	B. Pittaway	Waterton Park	
	G. L. Gladstone	Waterton Park	
	Jim Christiansen	Waterton Park	
Sept. 14	Marsh Gregg	Hungry Horse, Montana	Horse
	Leona Brown	East Glacier Park	

* * *

1954 Ranger Edward Olmstead

DATE	NAME	ADDRESS	TRANSPORTATION
May 27	Ed Olmstead	Glacier National Park	Saddle Horse
	Don Barnum	St. Mary, Montana	Saddle Horse
June 18	Dick Montgomery	West Glacier, Montana	Foot
July 20	Bill Yenne	West Glacier, Montana	Horse
July 27	Glen Burmuda	St. Mary, Montana	Horse
Aug 7	Bob Lechbutner	West Glacier, Montana	Foot
	John McMullen	Two Medicine	Foot
	Jack Bell	Cutbank, Montana (3)	Foot & 2 pack horses
	Hotel Help	Many Glacier (5)	Foot
Aug 9	Ed Risse, Jr.	West Glacier, Montana	Foot
Aug 22	Ken Bride	Many Glacier	Foot
	Dahl Davidson	Many Glacier	Foot
	Charles Young	Many Glacier	Foot
Sept. 4	J. M. Christensen	Waterton Park (3)	Foot

Sept. 13	Keith Robinson	East Glacier Park	Wagon
	Marjorie Gregg	Hungry Horse, Monta	Wagon
	Leona Brown	East Glacier Park	Wagon
Sept. 23	Don Barnum	St. Mary, Montana	Horse
	Grace Barnum	St. Mary, Montana	Horse
	Hugh Buchanan	St. Mary, Montana	Horse
	Madelyn Buchanan	St. Mary, Montana	Horse

* * *

1956 Ranger: Ed Olmstead

DATE	NAME	ADDRESS	TRANSPORTATION
May 21	Ed Olmstead	Glacier Nat'l Park	Foot
June 2	Andy Russell (5)	Waterton Townsite	5 Saddle Horse

* * *

1958 Ranger: Joe Heimes

DATE	NAME	ADDRESS	TRANSPORTATION
June 3	Joe Heimes	Babb, Montana	Saddle Horse
	Al Vail	St. Mary	Saddle Horse, 8 mules
June 13	Don Barnum	St. Mary	Saddle Horse
	Al Vail	St. Mary	Saddle Horse
July 1	Maude M Benson	East Glacier Park	Horse
	H. G. Benson	East Glacier Park	Horse
July 8	Al Kytomer	Waterton R. S. (15 yr. seasonal in Glacier)	Foot
July 16	Edward Mummel	Belly River	Horse
	Stan Joseph	N. P. S.	Horse
	Max E. Edgar	N. P. S.	Horse
	Don Barnum	N. P. S.	Horse
July 21	J. M. Christensen	Waterton Park	Horse
Aug 4	Gerald M. Richman	U. S. Geological Survey (4)	Foot
Aug 18	Mr. & Mrs. Benson	East Glacier Park	Jeep
Aug 19	Henry Benson	East Glacier Park	Wagon
	Maude Benson	East Glacier Park	Wagon
Sept. 12	Mr. & Mrs. Earl Siers	Babb, Montana	
	Grace & Don Barnum	St. Mary, Montana	
Sept 26	Henry Benson	East Glacier Park	Horse
Oct 4	Henry Benson	East Glacier Park	Horse
	Archie Sangador	East Glacier Park	Horse

* * *

1962 Ranger: Lou Hendricks

DATE	NAME	ADDRESS	TRANSPORTATION
Feb 27	William M Colony	West Glacier	Skis
	El Olmstead	East Glacier	Skis
	Bob Frauson	St. Mary	Skis
June 5	Chuck Bengtson	St. Mary	Pack String
June 14	Chuck Bengtson	St. Mary	Pack String
June 18	Chuck Bengtson	St. Mary	Pack String
June 20	Joe Keeler	Raymond	Pack String
Sept. 30	Louis A. Hendricks	Closed Station for 1962	
Oct 18	Louis A. Hendricks	with party of four surveyors, stayed at the station to survey for new buildings and sewer and water systems.	

* * *

BEAVER CURIOSITY by Brian McClung

During my younger years, I became so captivated with Joe Cosley and his trapping way of life. I even imagined that one-day I too would become a mountain man trapper. Beaver were spellbinding. I felt that if I could learn about the beaver way of life, I would somehow gain a deeper understanding of the famous Joe Cosley.

To show you some of the love I have for beaver, I have included the following short write-up.

I hope you are enthralled with beaver as much as I am. My pinnacle moment with beaver was to hold a white beaver in my arms.

Beaver *(castor fiber Canadensis)* are semi aquatic nocturnal rodents, the largest rodents in North America. They have fully webbed feet, which help in swimming, and a broad flat tail. Their fur is exceedingly fine and close. When freed of the long hairs, the thick dense fur next to the skin is one of the most valuable commercial furs.

My fascination with beavers started when I was a Boy Scout in Western Canada. I was assigned to the Beaver Patrol and was asked to do some research on beavers. I have continued to learn about beavers all my life.

Then trapping stories and famous local trappers like Joe Cosley captured my interest. Beaver soon fascinated me.

In my studies, I learned that most beavers are usually brown in color. In the cold country and high mountains of Alberta and Montana, beaver are a little darker brown, and the richer color brings higher prices. They are also larger and have heavier more dense fur.

Though rare, there are also red beaver and white beaver. The most highly prized skins are the very rare black beavers found in the Hudson Bay drainage system. They bring the highest prices at auctions everywhere.

The beaver is warm and dry even in the winter swimming beneath the ice on the beaver pond. Their coat consists of two layers. The outer layer is long coarse guard hairs and underneath next to the skin is the dense under fur. This fur is in prime condition towards the end of winter.

Beavers are in high demand for their valuable fur to make hats, coats or blankets. All parts of a beaver may be used.

Beavers use their castor to polish and protect their fur, to identify each other as members of the family, and to distinguish and attract the opposite sex when looking for a mate.

Like rodents everywhere, they have remarkable teeth. Their incisors grow continuously at a rapid rate throughout the animal's life span. If the beaver doesn't wear down its teeth by gnawing, the top incisors can grow back into the palette piercing the skull causing death. However, for the industrious beaver, this is seldom a problem. In beaver farms the teeth are cut back by saws.

As beaver cut trees down or trim off branches to be stored as food the teeth sharpen. Together with their powerful jaws, they can fell a tree in short order, about the same time a woodsman can with a sharp axe.

However big and sharp their teeth are, beavers are not aggressive to man or other creatures. If picked up, beaver will not bite back, but they do not like it. They avoid humans and slap their broad tails hard on the water to warn off anything not welcomed.

Tail slapping expresses resentment at an intruder and sounds like a rifle shot that may be heard a mile away. If you were to get close to a beaver in its pond, this sound can really put a scare into you and make you jump. Beavers resent the presence of any creature they perceive a threat that trespasses their domain.

Names and Sizes of Beaver

Age	Weight in Pounds	Name	Pelts Sizes
Birth	1	kit	
3 weeks	1½-2	kit	
6 weeks	4	kit	
1 year	25	yearling	small
2 years	35-40	sub adult	medium
3 years	50	adult	large
6 years	60-70	adult	blanket
Old animal	80-90	adult	large blanket
Record	110	adult	XXL blanket

Life expectancy for beaver is around fifteen years, but some have been tracked for twenty-two years.

Beaver seldom travel far from their home territory. They have been known to travel 600 yards but that is rare. Belly River beaver are most likely from Alberta, Canada.

Facts are facts, but let me share them in the context of life over a two-year cycle — The Year of the Beaver.

THE YEAR OF THE BEAVER

Busy As A Beaver

Dam building is an instinctive and irresistible reaction to the sound of rushing water and seeing the water level drop. However, the skills that make the beaver such a superb engineer must be practiced to be perfected. Repairs are set about quickly and efficiently. Small sticks are placed carefully in between larger ones to stop the water's flow. Usually it is only an emergency of this magnitude that will make a beaver leave its lodge during the day.

Early accounts suggest that the beaver was originally a daytime creature. The advent of the trappers drove the majority of these supremely adaptable animals to a nocturnal being, sleeping by day and leaving the lodge only under cover of darkness.

Using their teeth and claws beavers can create impressive structures — some twelve feet high and 600 feet long. A pair of beavers using mostly sticks and mud (substituting just about any material they can find) may build a substantial dam in three or four nights.

Far from randomly piling up twigs, beavers use the water line as a carpenter's level and adapt their design to the flow of the water and the natural features of the land. Work continues long into the spring evening until the situation is under control.

The beavers often linger in the pond until sunrise. They swim with easy grace propelled by powerful back legs. Broad flat tails maneuver them expertly through the pond. Beavers are superbly designed for under-water activity. Special valves close off their noses and ears, and thin membranes act as goggles for the eyes.

Preparations For Winter

The beaver lodge is made stronger than their dams. Their home is usually six or more feet higher than the water level. Inside, the beaver have carved out a large interior living area above, a dome-shaped chamber about two and a half feet high. The floor is a few inches above the water and is hard-packed dirt carpeted with shredded wood chips to make the floor clean and dry.

There are two underwater channels to and from the lodge. Their main or usual entrance is 15 inches in diameter, big enough to drag branches inside to eat. The other, a little smaller, is a means of escape in case of attack by a bear.

One special feature of every beaver lodge is the breathing hole that allows stale air outside and fresh air back in. When the lodge is occupied the moist air exhausting out this hole hits the winter weather turning it into steam.

As autumn approaches, beaver are preoccupied with gathering branches: cottonwood, alder, poplar and birch. Almost anything will do, though aspen is the favorite choice.

When the leaves turn color, there is a sharp increase in the pace of activity preparing for winter. Beavers are great providers of food storage for the entire winter season. The vital food supply is anchored to the floor of the pond and close to the entrance of the lodge to be readily accessible even in the coldest weather.

Beavers are aquatic rodents, spectacularly suited to their watery environment. The adult beaver can swim a quarter of a mile under water, but if it needs to, can hold its breathe for 15 minutes at a time. Under the ice they can breathe air that has been trapped between the water and the ice. Beaver can also recycle its breath and prolong their dives even further. However, the food storage is always located adjacent to the entrance to the lodge so trips under the ice are relatively short.

Each year the lodge is repaired and made higher and bigger for the up-coming winter season and the increased room parents think they will need. It must be ready to withstand the first winter storm.

Winter

By November the pond is beginning to freeze over. When the pond freezes over all work stops abruptly.

Winter soon settles in quietly, firmly, undeniably. The beavers are not only well stocked with a food supply, but also protected from the weather by their well-insulated dwelling. Now the lodge is further insulated by a deep blanket of snow.

The sticks and mud of the lodge freeze as solid as cement and provide a windproof shelter against the bitter cold. It also is strong enough to with stand the power of a grizzly trying to get a last tasty meal before hibernation.

Snug inside, the beavers are prepared for months of quiet isolation. From underneath the pile of lodge material they have cut a chamber with separate areas for eating and sleeping. Each lodge is a single family dwelling, housing a pair of beavers who mate for life, and their offspring.

The beaver leaves the lodge in the winter only when necessary. One by one the stored branches are carried home to be eaten in warmth and safety. Skin flaps behind the teeth allow the beaver to hold the branches without swallowing water. A well-mannered beaver sits on his haunches turning the branch like corn on the cob. Its sharp front teeth will strip away the bark in no time, leaving nothing but the woody core.

Beavers are strict but rather voracious vegetarians. They eat up to two pounds of food a day, swimming back and forth many times to raid the storage area.

Each time a beaver returns to the lodge the others use their keen sense of smell to reassure themselves that the animal is a member of this family. Secure, well-fed and warm the beaver enjoys an after dinner groom. The animals' combined body heat makes the interior of the lodge quite comfortable. But outside, the temperature has plummeted to 40 below zero.

For other animals outside the beaver's lodge, finding food becomes a full-time occupation. Those that don't survive will end up becoming meals for other starving animals.

Breeding varies with the altitude and age of the parents. In the Alberta and Montana mountains it occurs in late January or early February. Gestation period averages 110 days, so birth coincides with spring.

Beaver are gregarious, tending to associate with others of one's kind and growing in a cluster or colony.

Springtime in the Rockies

Spring is a good time for the beaver. The end of May an important annual event takes place in the beaver family.

Mother has carefully prepared a soft bed of shredded twigs where the young will stay warm and dry. Each newborn receives a thorough cleaning.

The litter can vary from 2 to 4 kits for young parents, to as many as 8 kits for older parents. The kits are born better than most rodents, fully furred with their eyes partially open and their teeth developed. The male helps the female through the labor period that may last as long as 60 hours.

The newborns start to groom themselves after about an hour. The kits emerge tail first. They can walk and swim immediately. But they float like a cork and cannot dive. Nor can they hold their breath long enough to exit the lodge.

They will nurse for several weeks, although they will begin taking solid food as well within the first few days.

The beavers keep their young within the safety of the lodge for several weeks until they are old enough to go outside. The parents rarely leave them unattended. An adult or yearling remains at home while the others go in search for food.

The young stay with their parents for close to two years learning the complex routines of beaver life. A yearling lives harmoniously with new brother and sister kits when they are born. Either the yearlings or the adults will keep the kits supplied with food and will baby-sit. This is a round the clock duty.

The adults or yearlings make trip after trip from the lodge to gather fresh twigs and grass. If there is still a little ice on the pond the adult will push up on the ice and break it so they can forage ashore for fresh food.

The yearlings are beginning to learn "to work like beavers." In spite of repeat trips, the little ones are always hungry. Their strident voices and cries can be heard at a considerable distance from the lodge.

The aspen trees are in full bloom providing a succulent meal of tender greenery after months of eating tough stored bark. The trees grow in such abundance now that finding food requires very little effort.

The warm sun encourages even the nocturnal beaver to bask a little in its gentle rays. Summer season is very near.

The new parent has not forgotten its responsibilities back at the lodge. The beaver is an unselfish animal. Each member of the family is amply provided for. The young are indulged -- allowed to nibble any branch they can reach. But their mother is still the most important source of food.

Throughout these early weeks the kits are awake both day and night in short busts of activity: exploring the lodge, fooling and playing and learning by imitating their parents and their older siblings). Their cries will lessen as they grow older but at this point they are quite vocal.

In less than three hours after birth the kits can float on the water. Two weeks later their swimming has improved but they still don't weigh enough to dive, nor do they have sufficient breath control to exit the lodge through the steeply angled tunnels. It will be some time before they can leave the safety of their home.

In the meantime, ever vigilant parents make sure the kits stay where they belong. They are weaned at approximately six weeks. During their first summer kits do little useful work.

Early Summer Routine

The sudden thaw places pressure on the beaver's dam. Giving way, the dam unleashes a torrential flood summoning the beavers from their lodge.

As the evening falls, the beaver family emerges from their lodge and begins the night's work. Using his incisors the father is about to fell an aspen. His assistant is his son born the previous spring. Across the pond is the mother absorbed in watching over her kits. This is their first excursion in the outside world. Close supervision is a must. She will keep them far from the half cut aspen. The whole family will be involved in the training and care of the young, but most of the duty goes to the mother. The father has other business to attend to.

By now the kits have become expert swimmers. They become accustomed to outdoor life quickly and enthusiastically. Still it will be many months before they can safely travel alone.

In the meantime there are other modes of transportation. Some kits ride on their mother's big tail, but not for long because she flips them off.

Strong jaws and chisel-like incisors make quick work of soft wooded trees. A five inch willow can be downed in about three minutes. Beavers have been recorded felling trees some three feet in diameter and 110 feet tall.

Activity intensifies as the hour advances; gathering food and modifying the dam to maintain the proper water level make up the bulk of the night shift. Sometimes beavers dig canals out from the pond to make access to food trees easier. They can then float branches down to the main pond rather than dragging them over land. By sunrise the beavers will be safely hidden inside their lodge where they usually remain until the next evening. By day the pond belongs to other creatures.

Lessons begin for beaver kits as they explore the pond and its surroundings. The parents or older siblings are constantly around to keep them out of trouble. They are getting better at negotiating challenges every day. The kits are capable of staying under water long enough to travel safely to and from the lodge. Already they propel themselves like tiny submarines.

Still they are far from perfecting the fine arts of beaver life. It will take many months of practice before they master the skills of tree cutting, branch harvesting and storage, and dam repair.

By the end of August the weather has turned unpredictable. Summer storms develop without warning. Heavy showers pound. Waves swell streams. Once more the dam gives way. The incident is serious and threatens to drain the beaver's pond. It is in the middle of the day and the beavers have retired to the safety of their lodge. The situation requires quick action in spite of the increased vulnerability to predators. While the father stays home to mind the kits, the mother and her yearling cope with the task: measure the damage, carefully replace sticks and plaster with mud — working tirelessly to save the pond. It is an important moment for the young beaver. He has observed his parents maintaining the dam for over a year but only now when danger threatens is he called upon to help. Happily he rises to the occasion. The pond is saved.

The beaver's behavior to maintain its dam is compulsive. Its instinct leaves it no other choice. But in its constant struggle against the elements, it provides food and shelter — the very stuff of life for others in its habitat.

The Second Spring Nears For The Yearlings

Another fall and another winter. The second breeding season passes as well. Spring is still a good month away but the beaver continues to fair well.

Beaver are very clean animals. As soon as the beaver returns inside the lodge it grooms itself. Oily liquid secreted from a gland near the base of its tail is rubbed into the undercoat. The oil helps repel the icy water and keeps the beaver warm and its skin dry on its foray into the pond.

In early April the days are growing longer at last. The sunlight lingers more each day and winter begins to loose its icy grip. Warmer days will liberate the wilderness and all its creatures. Melting snow will swell the dormant streams and rivers, bringing them to life.

In the spring, just before the next birthing, the yearlings are almost two years old. These subadults are well able to live independent lives. They are kicked out of the lodge for good and forced to leave the family dam. This accomplishes two things. 1) It gets the grown youth to strike out on its own and find a new home and look for a future lifetime mate, and 2) Makes more room in the lodge for the soon to be born kits.

Graduation Day

Being expelled from the pond is a graduation for this generation to commence their own lives. Schooling is complete and the new adult beavers advance to starting their own lives somewhere else. It takes several reminders from the parents before these new adults really get the message that they are being sent away never to return. They are now no longer welcome at home.

The early summer is the time to explore new territory and hopefully discover a mate. Beavers know what to do and make good use of the summer preparing for the winter ahead. A new stream must be located and dammed. A new lodge needs to be built and food stored for the upcoming winter.

If a new adult beaver does not find a mate, a lodge and dam will still be built. The search for a mate will intensify the following summer. Brothers or sisters will also start a new lodge and dam in the new location but as soon as a mate is found for one, the other sibling is asked to move on with their blessing.

However, if the new adult is successful in attracting a mate they will be ready to breed during the winter months inside the lodge. At age three the adults will then be parents for the first time.

The cycle of life has begun some distance from their birth home. The beaver colony continues to grown in population and area.

Generous, industrious and persevering, the beaver will continue to provide an irreplaceable service to its fellow creatures and for the land itself.

REFERENCES

Frank Goble, "The Trapper" Volumes 1, 2 & 3. Paperback. Lots of pictures of camps, the country and the trappers. Contains a detailed map to show you the way. It is factual, unembellished narrative written by one who was not only a trapper, but also a keen observer and an able writer. I heartily recommend all three volumes. The books can be order individually at $19 Canadian each or as a set for $59.00. The complete set is 380 pages of pure delight adventure on the trapline. Frank's phone is: (403) 653-3510

Julia Nelson, *"Cosley, Trapper and Guide Extraordinary,"* Part 1, Canadian Cattlemen, August 1953, p6,7,10,27. Part 2 September, 1953 p34,35,38. Also reprinted in the Chief Mountain Country: A History of Cardston and District. 1978, pp. 293-297.

Julia Mecham was born in Taber and moved to Mountain View in 1933 with her parents. The Nelson family homesteaded in Mountain View in the late 1800's. George Nelson, the oldest son, helped to support his parent's large family. He hunted and trapped, also with his older sister Sarah. Their main catches were muskrats and coyotes. They knew how to put up fur and deer, elk, moose and cattle hides. Indians frequented their home as did local ranchers with requests for furs to be put up or cured. George and Julia married in 1936.

Julia was talented in writing, music and reading. She taught piano in Beazer, Leavitt and back to Mountain View, riding this circuit on horseback. Julia's 1953 article was the most thorough work on Joe Cosley to that date. It was thrilling.

Jerome (Jerry) DeSanto, *"50 years in Glacier's back country . . .the legendary Joe Cosley,"* Montana The Magazine of Western History, Winter, 1980, p 11-27.

Jerry DeSanto is now a retired ranger for Glacier and Yellowstone National Parks. He was stationed in Joe Cosley's country in 1966.

His research on both sides of the border pushed the Joe Cosley Story the furthest. His work is very academic with footnotes and references to document every step of the Cosley Trail.

Jerry still spends time visiting the ranger station at Goat Haunt and summers in Southern Alberta when he is not living in Montana.

David Shea, *"Belly River: Packer's Paradise,"* Great Falls Tribune, Thursday, August 25, 1988, Outdoors Section. The article quotes Shea, "You don't know what a good horse is until you get one." I believe Heimes would understand just what Shea was talking about. David Shea named his 23 year old horse, "Irish John," and the article featured two pictures of Irish John with Shea at the Belly River Ranger Station.

Norton Pearl, *"Backcountry Ranger" in Glacier National Park*, 1910 - 1913. The diaries and Photographs of Norton Pearl. Edited and Annotated by Leslie Lee, 1994

Preserving History

There are many newspaper stories, magazine articles, letters and picture stories that Joe Cosley wrote or drew and had published that we just do not have today. If you know of any documents or photos, please share them with us.

We want to improve this book. The author's goal in revising this edition is to replace rumor with fact. If you find omissions or errors, please forward them to us.

We also encourage you to start writing your personal or family history. As we get older, we see the value of preserving special times and the need to put things in order before it is too late.

Send all correspondence to: **Brian and Marie McClung**
Life Preservers Publishing
2863 Jamie Rose Street
Las Vegas, NV 89135-2047

* * * *

Reflections by Joe Cosley
Taken from a letter to Mrs. Margaret Ivens, dated January 28th, 1935
My Dear Very Rich–Widow:-

"When all that matter, shall be written down
And the long record of your years is told,
What to your credit, shall you find inscrolled?
And what shall be the jewels of your CROWN?"

Ah, when I think of the above lines and "when the tombs close on our fair renown." my soul shivers with spiritual fright! Lon Scott and I thought this over as we reposed beneath a juniper tree in the North Fork of the Flathead River, on a sunny peaceful day, resting our horses. At the termination of our dream, I asked him what sort of crown shall he wear when he goes to kneel before the Angel who holds the book of each individual life record to hear of any good deed he might have rendered to some lonely one and such! I was serious, but he wasn't.

So the poor fellow is dead. I wonder if he thought of me in his dying state, of what I had said to him in that lonely spot and of the one who is going to pass out of the picture first of all.

LIFE PRESERVERS PUBLISHING
ORDER FORM

Please send the following books by Brian McClung:

____

____

____

Satisfaction Guaranteed

Please send more FREE information on:
□ Other Products □ Speaking Seminars □Consulting

Sales Tax:
No state sales tax please. Payable in US Dollars.

Shipping within USA: $7.00 US for first book and $3.50 for each additional product.

Payment:
❑ Check ❑ MasterCard and Visa
Card number:______________________________

Name: ______________________________

Address: ______________________________

____

Phone #: ______________________________

⊠ Postal orders: **Life Preservers Publishing LLC**
2863 Jamie Rose Street, Las Vegas, NV 89135
Phone or Fax Toll Free: 888-360-8162
We do not ship directly to Alberta or Montana.
Please order from the great Merchants listed on our website at Glacierparkbooksandvideos.com